James Maxton

£2

James Maxton

William Knox

Manchester University Press

Copyright © William Knox 1987

Published by Manchester University Press, Oxford Road,
Manchester, M13 9PL, UK
27 South Main Street, Wolfeboro, N.H. 03894-2069, USA

British Library cataloguing in publication data
Knox, William
  James Maxton. —(Lives of the left) 1. Maxton, James 2. Independent Labour
  Party—Biography 3. Politicians—Great Britain—Biography. 4. Socialists
  —Great Britain—Biography
  I. Title   II. Series
  941.082'092'4   DA566.9.M39/

Library of Congress cataloguing in publication data applied for

ISBN 0 7190 2152 7 *hardback*
ISBN 0 7190 2153 7 *paper*

Printed and bound in Great Britain by
Robert Hartnoll (1985) Ltd., Bodmin, Cornwall

Contents

LIVES of the LEFT is a new series of original biographies of leading figures in the European and North American socialist and labour movements. Short, lively and accessible they will be welcomed by students of history and politics and by anyone interested in the development of the Left.   *general editor*   David Howell

published: **J. Ramsay MacDonald**   Austen Morgan
James Maxton William Knox
Karl Kautsky Dick Geary

forthcoming, to include: **Big Bill Haywood** Melvin Dubofsky
A. J. Cook Paul Davies
Aneurin Bevan Dai Smith
Thomas Johnston Graham Walker
Eugene Debs Gail Malmgreen
R. H. Tawney Anthony Wright
Ernest Bevin Peter Weiler

For my mother

Acknowledgements

I should like to thank Pat Bradley, Judith Dunkerly, David Earnshaw, Conan Fischer, Duncan Leuchars, Andy MacDdonald, Frank McMahon, John Maxton MP, Anne Quinn, Drew Scott, Tracey Waters and not least my wife, Magi and son, David, for their help and encouragement. Special thanks must also go to Manchester University Press and the editor of the series, David Howell. The library staffs of the National Library of Scotland, the London School of Economics, the British Museum and the Strathclyde Regional Archives were helpful and friendly, making researching a pleasant experience. The whole project would have been impossible without the financial assistance I received from the Carnegie Trust for the Universities of Scotland, to whom I remain indebted.

Abbreviations

BSP	British Socialist Party
BUF	British Union of Fascists
CPGB	Communist Party of Great Britain
CNT	Spanish Anarcho-Syndicalist Union Federation
CWC	Clyde Workers' Committee
CWP	Common Wealth Party
EIS	Educational Institute of Scotland
GEA	Glasgow Education Authority
ILP	Independent Labour Party
LAI	League Against Imperialism
LRC	Labour Representation Committee
LSI	Labour and Socialist International
NAC	National Administration Council
NCF	No Conscription Fellowship
NEC	National Executive Committee
NGSW	Not Genuinely Seeking Work
NUWM	National Unemployed Workers' Movement
PLP	Parliamentary Labour Party
POUM	Partido Obrere de Unificación Marxista
RPC	Revolutionary Policy Committee
SCTA	Scottish Class Teachers Association
SDF	Social Democratic Federation
SHRA	Scottish Home Rule Association
SIOT	Socialism in Our Time
SL	Socialist League
SLP	Socialist Labour Party
STUC	Scottish Trades Union Congress
SWRC	Scottish Workers' Representation Committee
TA	Triple Alliance
TUC	Trades Union Congress
UFC	United Free Church
UIL	United Irish League
USSR	Union of Soviet Socialist Republics

1 *From blue to red*

History has not been kind to James Maxton. Reviled by contemporaries for leading the Independent Labour Party (ILP) out of the Labour Party in 1932, the attitude of later generations has been no more generous. The driving idealism of Maxton and his critique of the gradualism of the Labour Party has been given short shrift by those operating and writing within the pragmatic tradition of British politics. A. J. P. Taylor described his career as 'barren of achievement'.[1] Yet there is little doubt that Maxton was the outstandingly charismatic figure of the inter-war Labour movement. He was said by Fenner Brockway to have made more socialists than any other comparable figure in Britain, he was mentioned in the same breath as giants such as Keir Hardie, Eugene Debs and Karl Liebknecht and was thought of as the finest orator in the English-speaking world and a future leader of the Labour Party. There is then to many a lacuna between Maxton's actual and his potential achievement.

These differences among critics and admirers are in part the result of ideology and in part the consequence of Maxton's enigmatic character. A declared revolutionary, he was loved and fated as a parliamentary institution – Churchill described him as 'the finest gentleman in the House of Commons'; a leader who saw himself primarily as an agitator and a rebel. Maxton is not the conventional subject of political biography. Neither is he the man of ambition whose career was destroyed by some personal tragedy or weakness of character. Maxton saw his task in life as that of the unremitting politicisation of the masses in the direction of Socialism; all else was secondary. It is the success or failure in the pursuit of this goal which ought to form the proper context of history's verdict. The orthodox game of high politics and offices attained are not suitable criteria for assessing the contribution of Maxton to the British Labour movement, particularly when that contribution lay in the field of action and ideas as experienced by those inhabiting the lower slopes of British politics.

This short biography will seek to re-evaluate Maxton's career, hopefully free from the hagiographic approach of his close associates and the bias of his opponents. It will also attempt to establish the relevance of his ideas for us and examine the coherence of his strategy and tactics in the implementation of his political philosophy. Therefore, although heed must be paid to the narrative conventions of political biography, it is the ideas and political practice of Maxton which will form the main focus of this study.

2

Unlike a number of his Labour colleagues, Maxton was not the product of a working-class background. His father, John, and his mother, Melvina (née Purdon), were both school-teachers who had met and married while studying in Edinburgh. There were five children, of whom James was the second eldest. In time all became teachers, with Maxton's younger brother, John, achieving outstanding academic success as director of the Institute of Agrarian Affairs at the University of Oxford. At the time of Maxton's birth (22 June 1885) the family lived in a three-roomed house in Pollokshaws, an important residential suburb of Glasgow where Maxton senior was employed as an assistant master at Pollok Academy on a salary of £90 per annum. Things improved substantially when five years later John Maxton was appointed headmaster of Grahamston School, Barrhead.

Barrhead was, at that time, a self-contained little town about seven miles from Glasgow, noted for the production of sanitary appliances by the world famous Shanks and Co. It was here that Maxton began his formal education in his father's school. In 1900 he won his first scholastic prize for scripture at the Barrhead Free Church Sunday School. In the same year he won a three-year scholarship from Renfrewshire County Council to attend one of Scotland's most prestigious schools – Hutcheson's Grammar School. There he excelled at sports, particularly athletics and fencing, and passed the Hutcheson's Trust Scholarship examination which allowed him to continue his education as a pupil teacher on an annuity of £15. In 1902 Maxton's father died and his education was temporarily halted as he was forced to take a teaching post at the Martyr's Public School in the Townhead district of Glasgow. However, later that year, at his mother's insistence, Maxton entered the Glasgow Free Church Teachers' Training College and matriculated as a student at the University of Glasgow.

Maxton became actively involved in most aspects of undergraduate life. He was a member of the Students' Representative Council at Glasgow University and on the editorial committee of the *Glasgow University Magazine*, as well as being a sub-editor of the training college's student publication. Maxton also represented the university at athletics meetings gaining a reputation around Glasgow as a useful half-miler. When in later life his health deteriorated, Maxton retained his love of sport and was said to have been particularly fond of golf. During the vacations he found work in the Assessors' Office of Glasgow Town Council. However, his first entry into politics was as a member of the university's Unionist Association. As a young Tory, Maxton gave his support and vote to George Wyndham, Conservative Chief

Secretary for Ireland, in the Lord-Rectorship contest against the Liberal intellectual, John Morley, in 1903. Maxton also joined the university's 1st Lanarkshire Rifle Volunteers.

The Toryism of his early undergraduate days, Maxton later put down to political ignorance, claiming that he did not know the difference between the Liberal and Conservative Parties. However, it was perhaps more to do with the influence of his parents. His father was a Presbyterian with noted Unionist sympathies and a devotion to the Scots historian and philosopher, Thomas Carlyle, whose critique of the social consequences of early industrialisation was part of the philosophical make-up of Labour leaders such as Keir Hardie. But whether it was Carlyle the social critic or Carlyle the champion of conservatism who appealed to John Maxton is not known. Even though he was not an active Unionist, there is no evidence that Maxton's father was sympathetic to Socialist ideas, and, in spite of her reputation for open-mindedness, neither was Melvina Maxton. Growing up in this kind of environment could not but have affected Maxton's early political outlook. The idea of a third force in Scottish politics – Socialism – probably never occurred to him until a later date.

It would appear that, on entering university, Maxton was simply the conventional product of a lower-middle-class upbringing but there were soon signs that he was becoming restive with his complacent acceptance of the norms of Edwardian society. As an undergraduate, Maxton came into contact with some of the most gifted Scots of his generation. His friends included Walter Elliot, then a Fabian but later Conservative Secretary of State for Scotland in the 1930s, Tom Johnston, founder of the Glasgow *Forward* and later Secretary of State for Scotland in the Churchill coalition government, John Maclean, Marxist and first Bolshevik Consul to Scotland, and Hugh Reyburn, later professor of philosophy at Cape Town University. It was in discussions with such men, particularly Maclean, and as a result of his experience of the poverty of the Glasgow working class while working as a school-teacher (with which we will deal later) that Maxton's social and political horizons were broadened.

Maxton's political metamorphosis, away from Toryism towards Socialism, was part of a wider social phenomenon among the Edwardian middle classes. The outdated Victorian assumptions regarding state intervention, poverty and political democracy had come under increasing attack from academics, politicians and social investigators in the early 1900s. The middle classes were caught up in what Beatrice Webb called the 'consciousness of sin', which had emerged from the social paradox of glittering wealth amid widespread poverty and squalor. The social studies of Booth and Rowntree into the causes of poverty pointed to the failings of the market system. However, while most of the middle classes were prepared to stop short at the piecemeal state interventionism of New Liberalism, which offered social amelioration but left the socio-economic basis of inequality untouched, or follow the lead of Joe Chamberlain and others along the path of protectionism and Social Imperialism, Maxton went further. Through study and social observation, he came to the conclusion that only the socialisation of private property could put an end to the societal evils which so stirred the conscience of Edwardian society.

One example of Maxton's changing political attitude was his decision to transfer to the non-combatant ambulance section of the 1st Lanarkshire Volunteers; another was his regular attendance at the open-air political meetings held by John Maclean of the Social Democratic Federation (SDF) in Paisley. Maxton later claimed that it was Maclean who influenced him most and 'was responsible for his conversion to Socialism'. Contact with Maclean and the SDF led Maxton to read some of the classic Socialist texts such as Robert Blatchford's *Merrie England* and *Britain for the British*, Peter Kropotkin's *Fields, Factories and Work-*

5

shops, and the radical land reformer Henry George's *Progress and Poverty.* As a member of an informal university Socialist study group he was led to read the works of Marx. Maxton accepted Marx's analysis of Capitalist production and labour theory of value, but, as his later writings were to prove, he failed to either accept or understand Marx's materialist explanation of historical development.

3

Socialist politics at this time were dominated by the ILP. The party had been formed as the result of a meeting in Bradford in January 1893 of like-minded political organisations and trades unionists. Its object was to increase working-class representation in the Commons and to break the hold of the Liberal Party over the trades union movement. It was not a Marxist party but a radical reforming organisation motivated by the spirit of evangelical non-conformity and the desire to improve the moral and physical well-being of the working class. In Scotland, the early Socialist pioneers were inspired by Jesus, Shelley, Mazzini, Whitman, Carlyle and Morris. Few had read the works of Marx and most were content to study the works of Robert Burns and the Bible for their social and political inspiration. The ideological basis of the party was eclectic and membership included free traders, land reformers, single taxers, radical liberals, temperance advocates and Socialists. It was this political mish-mash, along with the trades unions, which provided the main impetus towards the foundation of the Labour Representation Committee (LRC) which, following the election of twenty-nine Labour MPs in the general election of 1906, became the Labour Party.

It was the task of the LRC to secure independent political representation for the workers in England and Wales but in Scotland it was the Scottish Trades Union Congress (STUC) which took the lead in this matter. On the instruction of the

1899 STUC, a Scottish Workers' Parliamentary Election Committee was set up in 1900 following a conference in Edinburgh. The delegates came from trades councils, trades unions and political organisations such as the ILP and SDF, as well as the Co-operative movement. However, the new organisation held little sway over the Scottish Labour movement in general, being too weak financially and having too few members. To co-ordinate activities more systematically, the Committee was renamed the Scottish Workers' Representation Committee (SWRC) in 1902 but this initiative was only relatively more successful. Some by-elections, as well as the 1906 general election, were contested under the aegis of the SWRC, with limited success. The main problem was that of divided loyalties. The SWRC had been formed in the same year as the LRC and Scottish trades unionists who were members of British unions were normally affiliated to the latter. To affiliate to the former would have meant double the subscriptions, which few unions were prepared to pay. There was also opposition to a Scottish organisation from within the hierarchy of the LRC. Ramsay MacDonald and others on the LRC executive had no desire to see the establishment of a separate Scottish Labour Party and in 1906 the SWRC was renamed the Labour Party (Scottish section) and this eventually gave way in 1912 to the Scottish Advisory Council of the Labour Party. With the Labour Party established as the national organisation of labour, the ILP had to accept that it was simply another affiliated body – something which was, in the long run, to prove very difficult.

Although in Glasgow smaller Socialist organisations existed, such as the SDF and the Socialist Labour Party (SLP), and were active in the engineering workshops and the shipyards of the Clyde, it was the ILP which more accurately reflected the political economy of the working class and, consequently, posed a greater long-term threat to the hegemony of the Liberal Party in the

7

west of Scotland. However, the process was by no means automatic. The Scottish Liberals proved to be as radical as the ILP
and, in some cases, even more so, supporting such demands as
the eight hour day, the Employers' Liability Act and so on. The
Liberal-dominated Glasgow Town Council was to the forefront
of municipal Socialism. Utilities such as gas, water, electricity,
tramways and telephones were all under public ownership. The
Times in 1902 singled out Glasgow in a series of leading articles
as the centre of the experiment in municipalisation. The ILP was
not, therefore, as distinguishable from the Liberal Party in Glasgow as it was in places like Lancashire and Yorkshire. Moreover,
the large Irish presence in the west of Scotland also ensured that,
as long as the Liberals held out the promise of Home Rule for
Ireland, the United Irish League (UIL) would deliver the Irish
Catholic vote, which further inhibited the rise of Labour.

To undermine the Liberal hegemony, the Glasgow ILP
shrewdly concentrated on local issues, the most important of
which was housing. Glasgow's housing was among the worst in
Europe. According to the 1911 Census, over sixty-two per cent
of Glasgow's population lived in one or two roomed dwellings;
in England and Wales the comparable figure was eight per cent.
If we use the official standards for measuring overcrowding; that
is, three persons to a room, then over two-hundred thousand
people, or one-fifth of Glasgow's population, were living in over-
crowded conditions. In such circumstances infant mortality, ill-
health and disease were unacceptably high. Overall the death
rate was twenty per thousand, the tuberculosis rate was 1.5 per
thousand; and the infant mortality rate was one-hundred and
thirty-five per thousand – the highest in Britain. Of course, in
Glasgow's poorer areas the situation was much worse. Blackfriars
boasted an infant mortality rate of one-hundred and seventy-eight
per thousand and a tuberculosis rate of 3.5 per thousand. It was
not for nothing that James Stewart, ILP town councillor, stated

that 'Glasgow is earth's nearest suburb to hell'.

Most of the dwelling units were privately owned by small landlords, who dominated council politics. This fact was exploited by the ILP, who offered to build £8 cottage homes for workers out of the municipal tramways' profits. ILPers like Wheatley, Maxton and Johnston were able to equate the agricultural landlords of the Scottish Highlands and rural Ireland with the urban landlords and draw support from the immigrant communities' residual hatred for the former. Anti-landlord propaganda was bolstered by the Catholic Socialist Society and by the founding of the Highland Land League. The latter gave support to the crofters of the western Highlands in their struggle for land reform. There was also some success in reaching the trades unions. The Taff Vale judgement of 1902, which made secondary picketing an action in restraint of trade and hence the trades unions liable for damages, encouraged the unions to think of independent class representation in parliament. As a direct result of the 1902 judgement, the unions flocked to join the Labour Representation Committee (LRC) – the forerunner of the Labour Party. This trend was naturally reflected at local level. The Glasgow Trades Council (GTC) played a prominent part in the ILP-dominated Workers' Municipal Election Campaign. The crucial issue was, however, the 1908 economic slump, which created widespread poverty and distress among skilled and unskilled workers alike. The Glasgow ILP and SDF held demonstrations against unemployment and used these occasions to criticise the charitable and emigrationist schemes put forward by the Liberals as a solution to the crisis but, significantly, it was the ILP, and not the SDF, which showed itself more capable of mobilising protest. By 1914 the ILP had eighteen town councillors in Glasgow and a rapidly growing membership.

9

4

Perhaps it was the greater success of the ILP in reaching the workers that persuaded Maxton to join it and not the SDF but, according to his biographer, John McNair, the decisive moment was hearing Phillip Snowden speak in Glasgow. It was Snowden's oratory that 'definitely' made up his mind to become a member of the more moderate ILP. In spite of opposition from his mother, Maxton joined the Barrhead branch of the ILP in 1904 and almost immediately found himself elected Branch Literature Secretary. A few weeks later he was speaking at outdoor meetings. Before long Maxton was addressing meetings on a nightly basis and two or three times at weekends. Despite his subsequent election to the Commons, the habit was maintained for much of his adult life. An example of his work for the ILP can be seen in his schedule for a typical fortnight in the summer parliamentary recess of 1927. 'Since I left Blackpool, I have visited London, Govanhill, Bridgeton, Yoker, Cheltenham, Yeovil, Newton Abbot, Warrington, Lowestoft, Burnley, Nelson, Lanark and Rochdale'. This would seem to put paid to the myth spread by his opponents in the Labour movement that he was 'lazy'. Intellectually he was perhaps lazy but no one can argue that his propaganda work for the ILP was anything less than prodigious. Maxton, along with close associates like Patrick Dollan, first Catholic Lord Provost of Glasgow, spoke on street corners and toured the mining villages of Lanarkshire putting the ILP point of view. Dollan once remarked that in those pioneering days Maxton and he did not consider a meeting worthwhile unless they sold 200-300 pamphlets.

Maxton blossomed early as a propagandist and his oratorical abilities made sure of advancement within the ILP. A few years after joining the party he was elected to the secretaryship of his branch and the Renfrewshire ILP Federation, which he also represented on the Scottish Divisional Council. In 1912 he was elected Scottish representative on the ILP's National Administrative Council (NAC) and in the years 1913-19 served as Chairman of the Scottish ILP. Membership of important party committees saw Maxton rubbing shoulders with big names like Kier Hardie, Phillip Snowden, Ramsay MacDonald and Robert Smillie. By 1910 he had also formed an important and lasting friendship with John Wheatley, former miner turned businessman and newspaper proprietor. It was a partnership which was to prove profitable to both men. Maxton was the charismatic orator; Wheatley the shrewd and practical politician. The relationship was complementary. Without Maxton, Wheatley would never have achieved eminence in Labour politics, nor would his schemes have gained so much support among the rank and file. Contrastingly, without Wheatley's advice and guidance Maxton would have ended his days as just another orator; outstanding maybe but, like miners' leader A. J. Cook, lost in the political wilderness.

Politically, Maxton took part in a number of important campaigns prior to the First World War. He spoke in favour of the suffragette movement and took part in the struggle against the Osborne judgement of 1910, which made it illegal for trades unions to give financial support to political parties. The Osborne judgement threatened to strike a decisive blow at the future progress of the Labour Party which relied on support from the unions. Alongside Keir Hardie and other Labour leaders, Maxton spoke at countless meetings against the judgement. The Labour movement eventually succeeded in pressurising the Asquith government to rescind the judgement in 1913. Maxton also involved himself in the work of the Socialist Sunday Schools in Glasgow. The Schools were a response to the middle-class bias of the Scottish churches and their lack of social awareness. However, they represented an important network for establishing contacts with other Labour leaders as almost all of those of note in the Glasgow Labour movement were involved at some point in their lives. Although Maxton's political activities were more important to him, his work in the trades union movement was also a significant influence on his actions at this time.

5

Around the time of joining the ILP, Maxton was forced to quit university and earn his living as a teacher in Pollokshaws Academy. He later enrolled as a part-time student and in 1910 graduated from Glasgow University with an MA degree. Prior to that he resumed his acquaintance with John Maclean when both men were involved in teaching evening continuation classes in Pollokshaws. Maxton and Maclean devised a course under the title of 'Citizenship and the Social Sciences', using Marx's *Capital* as the set text. Needless to say, when the educational authorities got to hear of this the class was abruptly ended and it would seem that, apart from assisting briefly as a tutor in Maclean's Marxist economics classes in Glasgow's Central Hall, Maxton had little to do with Maclean after this incident. Political separation was no doubt the outcome of Maclean's orthodox Marxist position which opposed the reformism of the ILP and advocated revolutionary Socialism as the only solution to the socio-economic problems thrown up by Capitalist society.

After three years at Pollokshaws, Maxton was transferred to St James' School, Bridgeton, one of the most deprived areas in Glasgow. In these areas of extreme poverty, teachers worked under intolerable burdens for low wages and poor conditions of service. Maxton himself provides a graphic description of conditions at St James': 'In the school I was teaching I had a class of sixty boys and girls of about eleven years of age. . . thirty-six out of the sixty could not bring both heels and knees together because of rickety malformations'.[2] It was the poverty of the children and its deleterious effect on their mental and physical development which Maxton later said was an important factor in 'bringing me into the Socialist and Labour movement'. It was the indifference of the authorities to the dreadful conditions under which teachers had to labour that caused him to campaign for reform of the Scottish educational system.

Emulating his father, who was in his day President of the Renfrewshire branch of the Educational Institute of Scotland (EIS), Maxton became deeply involved in the work of the Scottish teaching unions. There were two important bodies representing the interests of Scottish teachers; the long-established but rather conservative EIS and the more recent but smaller and radical Scottish Class Teachers' Association (SCTA). In the few years before the outbreak of the First World War Maxton was elected onto the national councils and Glasgow district committees of both unions. Additionally, he served at various times as Treasurer, Secretary and Vice-President of the Glasgow district of the SCTA. He was also a founder member of the Glasgow Socialist Teachers' Association, which acted as a rank and file pressure group within the EIS, and as a recruiting agent among teachers for Socialism.

Maxton's campaign revolved around three main issues: the decentralised control of education, the size of classes and the pay and service conditions of teachers. He advocated amalgamating existing school boards in five authorities serving the whole of Scotland. This would encourage the standardisation of working conditions and create a simplified negotiating structure. In terms of pay, Maxton felt that the supply of teachers ought to be regulated to fit the actual demand, which would prevent wages from being forced down through excessive competition among teachers for work. Under the new system, salaries were to rise to £80-£250 a year for women and £100-£300 for men, with improved sick pay. Teachers would also be expected to teach fewer pupils. Maxton envisaged a recognised quota of not more than eight-hundred pupils per school and a maximum class roll of forty.

Maxton shifted his position on the question of female salaries and in 1914 supported a resolution at the Glasgow district meeting of the SCTA in favour of equal salaries for male and female teachers. In the same year he also called on the EIS to adopt a uniform salary scheme for all teachers and uniformity in the length of training. This was all part of Maxton's desire to create a well-paid, well-organised teaching profession. However, the realisation of these goals depended, he argued, on the thorough-going restructuring of union policy. Maxton advocated increased union subscriptions to build up a fighting fund in the event of industrial action and the implementation of a closed shop policy. Although he did not 'believe' in strike action by teachers, Maxton thought that it was legitimate for those union members involved in teaching evening school to withdraw their labour. Also, to improve solidarity, teachers found guilty of strike-breaking were to be expelled from the union.

The main focus of Maxton's attack was the school boards. A fair number of them were in the control of small businessmen more interested in holding down the rates than in improving educational facilities for the young. Towards the end of 1912 Maxton led a campaign against Paisley School Board, which was notorious among school boards for low salaries and poor working conditions. Maxton's first piece of journalism was an article in *Forward* on 21 December 1912 criticising the cartel Paisley had set up with other Renfrewshire boards to prevent a teacher leaving one board to take up employment with another in her/his first year of service unless approval was given by the original employer. The agreement was condemned by Maxton in the strongest possible terms. He claimed that Paisley School Board 'have only made an indifferent copy of the methods more perfectly carried out by. . . Coates and Clark [textile manufacturers] which made Paisley what it is – a miserable, slave-driven, charity-ridden imitation of a third class Scottish burgh'. With public support the teachers forced the dissolution of the school board cartel and there followed a gradual improvement in the conditions of teachers in Renfrewshire schools. However, real improvements in the Scottish educational system were still some way off. All Socialists could do in the meantime was to stand as candidates in school board elections and hope to improve matters if elected but, since the elections were determined more by one's religion than one's class, Socialists were often the losers in these elections to sectarian candidates.

Maxton's growing Socialist awareness and his struggles to reform the Scottish educational system were leading him to develop a Socialist philosophy of education and to link this with an overall societal perspective. To him, a child was not a malleable piece of plastic to be moulded and shaped in the interest of capital and the state but a living organism whose growth, mental and physical, depended on the right amount of intellectual and material nourishment. Schools inside Capitalist society, Maxton argued, were 'dull, barracky, ugly places', more like 'prisons' than centres of learning. Education was another form of repression experienced by the working class. As Maxton put it: 'The existing system of industrial capitalism based upon the virtual subjection of the whole of the working class prevented, not only the development of the educational system. . . but any other form of social and political emancipation.'[3]

The repressive nature of the educational system was the reason Maxton (later) refused to send his son, James, to school until he was twelve years old and Maxton's sisters, Ada and Annie, took on responsibility for him until he reached that age. Real education, which Maxton considered to be the fullest development of the human personality, could only come about through the political emancipation of the working class. Thus he resolved to 'devote all his life and energy to the task of socialist propaganda'.

By 1914 Maxton's political transformation had been completed; the Unionist sympathies of his parents and his early days at Glasgow University had been abandoned and replaced by the political programme of the ILP. This metamorphosis had been the outcome of a conjuncture of forces of intellectual, material and political origin. His outstanding oratorical qualities had ensured a rapid rise in the political and trade union wings of the Labour movement. However, although he had become prominent in the Scottish ILP and the teachers' unions, Maxton was still largely unknown outside the west of Scotland. It took the train of events set off by the First World War to change him from a relatively obscure activist into a figure of national importance and popularity.

2 Red Clydeside

1

The declaration of war in August 1914 and the enthusiastic response of the workers shattered any illusions Socialists may have had regarding international working-class solidarity. Nationalism proved to be a more potent political force than Socialism, overriding class loyalties and uniting all political parties and social groups in common cause. The Labour movements of the major European countries lined up in support of the ruling classes in the supposed war to end all wars. Kitchener's slogan 'Your country needs you' sparked off a flood of voluntary enlistments in Britain, with the Scots response proportionately higher than the English. By February 1915 it was estimated that one in five Scottish miners had enlisted and that recruitment on the Clyde at twenty-four in every thousand of the male population was higher than in any other comparable industrial area of Britain. Nationally the Labour movement had declared in favour of entering into an electoral and industrial truce with the Asquith government. This led to the inclusion of some Labour leaders in the government and, with the change of prime minister in December 1916, Henderson accepted Lloyd George's invitation to join the War Cabinet.

In Scotland the political response of Labour to the war was no less favourable. Among Glasgow's eighteen Labour councillors, only two – John Wheatley and John S. Taylor – spoke out against the war and the GTC's pro-war faction was powerful enough to block participation by the Council in peace demonstrations. In Edinburgh the trades council supported voluntary recruitment and 'rendered valuable assistance to various local [military] units'. Thus repeating the pattern of the Boer War, the anti-war protestors and pacifists were, at the onset of hostilities, an unpopular minority. Yet only a few years later the *Scottish Review* could remark: 'The strength of the hostility to militarism in Scotland may be gathered from the fact that the War Party is a discredited minority in nearly all the Trades and Labour councils north of the Tweed.'

Such a remarkable turnabout in the fortunes of the anti-war movement represents a conjuncture of different forces, movements and personalities which created for a short time a fusion of the industrial and political struggle and in Glasgow gave rise to the enduring notion of 'Red Clydeside'. In this turbulent period Maxton was to play an important, if not decisive, role.

2

When war broke out, Maxton was still employed as a schoolteacher although he had since moved from St James' to Haghill Public School and then to Finnieston Public School – his final teaching post. In spite of the nature of his employment, Maxton spoke out against the war, viewing it in the same way as other ILP dissidents such as Hardie, MacDonald and Snowden did; as the outcome of Imperialist rivalries and secret diplomacy. But his opposition, like that of the ILP in general, was somewhat ambiguous. In the columns of *Forward* (24 October 1914) he urged the Socialist movement not 'to be swallowed up in a war or peace propaganda, but continue to conduct the business of Socialist manufacturing'. At the same time, he wrote to the *Educational News* (30 October 1914) complaining that unlike doctors, clergymen and veterinary surgeons, who all received a commissioned rank on enlistment, the War Office was only prepared to offer teachers the rank of corporal. Maxton demanded that this professional anomaly be taken up by the EIS and representation be made to the War Office and the Scottish Education Department with a view to its abolition. Again on 7 November 1914, Maxton at a meeting of the SCTA, tried to block the payment of a grant of £250 by the Association to the Scottish Teachers' Fund for War Relief. It was not, however, the giving that he attacked but the administration of the Fund. Maxton thought it was wrong to send indiscreet people to ask those in distress 'the most outrageous questions'.

His opposition to the war became firmer as the casualties mounted and discontent increased but at no time did he see in the war the opportunity to provoke a crisis in the state through the massive intensification of class struggle, thus speeding the revolutionary transformation of society onto a Socialist basis. Despite sharing platforms with revolutionary Socialists, Maxton and the Clydeside ILP's main criticism of the war was that it was being made an occasion for profiteering. At a war workers' conference sponsored by the Scottish miners on 20 February 1915, Maxton attacked the Labour Party for supporting a war which had given 'the speculators a unique opportunity of plundering the workers' and called Henderson 'a distinguished recruiting agent' for the Asquith government. It was an end to profiteering and the socialisation of the war effort, as well as a peace settlement with Germany, which constituted the programme of the ILP in the west of Scotland.

3

The first rumblings of domestic discontent with the war were heard in the shipyards and engineering shops of the Clyde. In February 1915 engineering workers struck for a 'tuppence' an hour increase in wages. Since the official union leadership was compromised by the industrial truce, the strike was declared unofficial. This allowed left-wing shop stewards, many of whom had syndicalist sympathies and advocated workers' control of industry, to take control of the strike. The shop stewards established a Central Labour Withholding Committee to press the (ultimately successful) claims of the engineers for a rise in wages. The experience gained in this struggle by the workers was to prove invaluable in the much larger campaign against the introduction of the provisions of the Munitions Act of June 1915. Essentially a measure to boost the production of armaments and other war-related materials through the introduction of unskilled labour on work previously the preserve of skilled men, by additions the legislation took the form of industrial conscription. The main cause of worker dissatisfaction was the implementation in August 1915 of a system of leaving certificates. David Kirkwood, a leading shop steward and member of the ILP, described the legislation as a 'slave's clause' as under it, workers could only leave their employment with the permission of their boss. It was in response to measures such as these that the Clyde Workers' Committee (CWC) was set up. The CWC conducted a number of strikes against the skill-dilution schemes and the system of leaving certificates.

The situation on Clydeside became an enveloping one as the industrial unrest was supplemented by the rent strikes of that year. Glasgow landlords had used the high earnings of munitions workers as an excuse to raise rents. The increases hit hardest at those women whose husbands were at the front or had been invalided out of the fighting. A spontaneous protest erupted among the Glasgow housewives against the rent increases, the evictions of serving or wounded soldiers' families and the high cost of food. The ILP was able to link these protests with their attacks on capitalist profiteering and as such it was they, and not the revolutionaries, who assumed the leadership of the rent strikes. John Wheatley and radical lawyer E R Mitchell threatened to fight so many strikers' cases against eviction and non-payment of rent in Glasgow Sheriff Court that the legal system was in danger of total paralysis. The campaign was so successful that the government was forced to pass the Rent Restrictions Act of December 1915, which froze rents at pre-war levels. This Act was a major step in the destruction of the free market in urban rents and had the political effect of identifying Labour more closely with housing reform in the eyes of the Glasgow working class.

The growing civilian unrest on Clydeside was of increasing concern to the Asquith government. To assuage the fears of the engineering workers over dilution, Lloyd George, Minister of Munitions, was sent to Glasgow to address them on the subject. Speaking on Christmas Day at St Andrew's Hall, the minister was given a hostile reception by the workers. *Forward* which reported the meeting – the only paper to do so – was suppressed and only allowed to resume publication after the editor, Tom Johnston, had assured Lloyd George that he would not publish anything guaranteed to prejudice the war effort. The suppression of *Forward* was the beginning of a series of measures aimed at the destruction of the CWC and the anti-war movement on the Clyde.

Failing to calm the fears of the workers and finding the demands of the shop stewards for workers' control of industry unacceptable, the authorities acted swiftly. The journal of the CWC – the *Worker* – was suppressed after only four issues for the alleged publication of a seditious article entitled 'Should the workers arm'. The chairman of the CWC, Willie Gallacher, along with John Muir and Walter Bell, was arrested and charged with sedition, in spite of the fact that the article was an attack on the idea of armed insurrection by the workers to overthrow the state. The arrests were a measure of the government's determination to break the CWC and isolate the revolutionary vanguard.

There quickly followed the arrest and deportation of the leading
shop stewards in March 1916, an event which was to lead to the
arrest and imprisonment of Maxton.

4

Voluntary recruitment came to an end in March 1916 with the
passing of the Military Service Act. A wide range of political
opinion was opposed to conscription and it was given organisational expression with the founding of the Liberal-inspired No
Conscription Fellowship (NCF). Maxton was already a member
of the Union of Democratic Control which was set up by E. D.
Morel and others to oppose secret diplomacy. However, as Scottish representative on the NCF, he was brought into contact
with radical Liberals and, more significantly, with the rising stars
of the ILP – Fenner Brockway, Clifford Allen and C. H. Norman
– who were greatly to shape the destiny of the party in the
1920s. As a conscientious objector to war, Maxton was ordered
to appear before Barrhead Military Tribunal. To testify to his
long-held Socialist convictions and his opposition to war, Maxton
called four witnesses – John Maclean, James MacDougall, William
Stewart and a town councillor. Maxton explained his political
pacifism to the Tribunal and assured them that, whatever hap-
pened, he would continue to oppose the war. Indeed, Maxton
and other Socialists had spoken at a great number of outdoor
meetings, many of which were broken up by patriotic gangs. In
1915 he accompanied an ailing Keir Hardie to the ILP's Easter
conference in Norwich which local patriots tried unsuccessfully
to smash by stirring up antagonism among the soldiers billeted
there. He also pointed out that his position as assistant master
at Finnieston School had been ended by the Glasgow School
Board because of his anti-war stand. The Tribunal accepted the
genuineness of Maxton's convictions and offered him the opportunity to join the Royal Army Medical Corps but he refused. On

his refusal the Tribunal delayed making a decision for two weeks until they discovered whether they had the power to grant him absolute or only conditional exemption. In the event his status was upheld. This answers the rather scurrilous suggestion of Willie Gallacher in his autobiography, *Revolt on the Clyde*, that Maxton went to prison to avoid conscription. Indeed, the Maxton family suffered doubly as his brother, John, was also imprisoned as a conscientious objector, firstly in Leeds and later in Wormwood Scrubs, London.

Between the time of adjournment and the date set for his re-appearance at the Tribunal, Maxton was arrested and charged with sedition under the Defence of the Realm Act. On 26 March he had spoken at a meeting in Glasgow Green, along with James MacDougall of the British Socialist Party (BSP), in protest against the deportation of David Kirkwood and other leading shop stewards. At the meeting Maxton declared that 'It is now time for the workers to take action and that action is to strike, to go home and forget to wind up your alarm clocks and down tools. . . In case there are any plain clothes detectives in the audience I shall repeat that statement. The men should strike and down tools.'

Four days later at his home in Barrhead, Maxton was arrested and taken to Duke Street Prison. After pleading not guilty to a charge of sedition before Sheriff Lyall in Glasgow Sheriff Court, Maxton and his fellow prisoner, MacDougall, were sent for trial at the High Court in Edinburgh. The date was set for 11 May.

During the period before his trial efforts were made to secure his release on bail. Ben Shaw, on behalf of the Scottish Advisory Council of the Labour Party, wrote to the Prime Minister, the Secretary of State for Scotland and the Executive of the Labour Party pleading Maxton's case, but with no success. Bail was turned down. In Duke Street Prison Maxton was treated fairly well; he received food prepared outside prison and mail from his close friends and relatives, although his letters to them were heavily censored. Despite the activities of the censor Maxton was able to write to his mother explaining why his principles had driven him to gaol. He wrote:

> I have done everything that I have done in the last years on principles which are greater and more fundamental than those which brought the panic legislation which has landed me in here. I'll be quite prepared to repeat the speech that I am charged on to any unprejudiced group of men after the war and get their verdict. It perhaps erred from the patriotic point of view, but not from the world-wide humanitarian view nor even the national view.

The trial, however, proved something of a humilation for both Maxton and MacDougall and called into question their militant convictions. The charge against them was that they had, on 26 March 1916 at Glasgow Green, urged the civilian population present, among whom were men engaged in the production of munitions and/or war materials, to strike and thus impede the production of munitions and war materials. On the advice of their counsel, both of the accused changed their plea to guilty and threw themselves on the mercy of the court. The defence was careful to emphasise the defendants' youth and the fact that both held responsible positions – Maxton in the teaching unions and MacDougall in local government. Counsel argued that it was the deportation of the shop stewards rather than the war which 'aroused [their] feelings' and 'coloured their speeches'. In the heat of the moment 'they had said what they had never previously said in their speeches'. Maxton and MacDougall followed this with an apology to the court and asked the Lord Justice General to take into consideration the 'regret they now felt at their quite inexcusable action' when passing sentence.

They were hardly the words of revolutionary Socialists but then none of the Clydesiders, with the exception of Maclean, displayed any contempt for the authority of the courts. Sentencing them, the judge described their action as one of 'dastardliness and cowardliness'. However, taking into account their apology, he passed what he considered a lenient sentence. Maxton and MacDougall were each given twelve months' imprisonment in Ediburgh's Calton Jail – the sentence to run from the date of apprehension. Calton Jail was one of the most authoritarian and inhuman prisons in Scotland. It was opened in 1816 and most of the cells were like small dungeons. There was no association work and prisoners were kept in solitary confinement for long periods, the only breaks from which were the daily exercise hour and attendance at religious service on Sundays. The diet was also monotonous consisting of bread, porridge and water, with occasional soup. It was here that the industrial and political vanguard of the Clyde were held. Sharing what Maxton jokingly referred to as his 'ancestral home' were John Maclean and James Mac-Dougall of the BSP, John Muir of the SLP, Willie Gallacher of the CWC, Arthur Woodburn of the ILP and some other anti-war protestors.

Maxton was given a job as a joiner repairing stools and tables. His easy-going manner and sense of humour endeared him to the warders and through discussion he was able to convince some of them to join the ILP and set up a branch of the Police and Prison Warders' Union. Although the meanness of the diet took its toll on Maxton's general health and was responsible for a severe illness which followed his release, his cheerfulness shielded him from the mental anguish suffered by Maclean, MacDougall and Muir. Maxton remained in good spirits in spite of his ordeal. In Duke Street Prison he had sent a light-hearted message to the ILP's April 1916 Conference apologising for his absence, saying that he was 'very sorry that [he] was not able to be with [them]. . . at Newcastle. . . as [he was] confined to [his] room'.

While in prison, his case, which had been left in abeyance by

25

the Glasgow School Board, was referred to a full meeting on 22 June 1916. A Tory member of the board moved that, in accordance with the terms of the Public School (Scotland) Act of 1882, Maxton be dismissed from the service of the board. George Hardie, half-brother of Keir, defended Maxton, arguing that the motion was politically inspired and that it was Maxton's abilities as a teacher and not his political views that the board members should take into account in coming to a decision. At the end of the debate the original motion was carried but without the necessary majority to make if effective, so the matter was adjourned for a further six months. However, Maxton never returned to teaching. Released from gaol on 3 February 1917, he was again called to appear before the Barrhead Military Tribunal and asked to take up work of national importance. Maxton refused to aid the war effort, even in the most indirect way. Eventually he was found work by John Scanlon as a plater's labourer with a firm of barge builders for neutral countries. He continued to protest against the war and was active in support of the Womens' Peace Crusade.

5

Maxton's release from prison coincided with the February Revolution in Russia. The news of the event was welcomed enthusiastically at the ILP Conference that April. The idea of workers' and soldiers' soviets captured the imagination of even ILP moderates like Ramsay MacDonald. This led to the Workers' and Soldiers' Convention in Leeds two months later at which Maxton, as chairman of the Scottish ILP (1913-19), was a delegate. However, the Convention proved to be more a popular demonstration of support for the Russian people than a serious attempt to emulate their political action. Several resolutions were passed favouring the regional organisation of soviets. One was set up in Glasgow but it seems to have collapsed because the town council wouldn't provide it with a hall to hold its meetings in! In any case, few in the ILP understood the significance of the soviets in Russian politics and fewer still had any idea of how to link it with existing working-class organisations. As John Wheatley remarked, 'Everyone pointed to the Russian road, but none was ready to lead the way'. The whole idea was quietly forgotten.

Maxton's labouring job brought him into contact once more with the CWC and allowed him to play an active part in its revival. After some years of industrial peace, the militant shop stewards were able to re-establish themselves as the authentic voice of the industrial working classes on Clydeside by leading the struggle against the Military Service Bill. The new legislation was aimed at ending the system whereby exemption from military service was granted on occupational grounds. The wholesale slaughter on the western front had forced the military authorities to widen their net in the search for manpower. Sir Auckland Geddes addressed the shop stewards on the new Bill in Glasgow's City Hall on 28 January 1918. Equalling Lloyd George's inept performance of 1915, Geddes allowed Gallacher and other militants to take control of the meeting. Arthur McManus, leading shop steward and, later, founder member of the CPGB, moved a resolution opposing the Bill and called for workers to bring the war to an end. Speaking as a representative of the CWC and a shipyard worker, Maxton seconded the resolution. He labelled the legislation a 'Manslaughter Bill' and drew the attention of the audience to the appalling level of war casualties which, he argued, was the result of the incompetency of the general staff. In spite of opposition from the official trades union officials, the McManus resolution was carried. This action signalled a move to the left in the trades union movement which culminated in the Forty Hours Strike of January/February 1919.

The promise of electoral success in the general election of November 1918, however, focused attention for a short period on mainline parliamentary politics. There were, in fact, distinctly positive signs to underscore the optimism of the Labour movement. The ILP, despite its record of opposition to the war, was growing rapidly in income and members. According to its own figures, membership in Scotland, which had stood at 5,656 in June 1918, had increased to 8,904 in September 1918 and the number of branches in the same period had grown from 184 to 192. Overall, the war years had witnessed a fifty per cent rise in the number of branches and a 300 per cent increase in membership. By September 1918 Scotland was the largest ILP region and, of 8,904 members, 2,000 were situated in Glasgow, where Bridgeton was the largest branch.

While in Calton Jail, Maxton was adopted as prospective parliamentary candidate for Bridgeton, although he had already been accepted as candidate for John Morley's old constituency, Montrose Burghs, in 1914. Bridgeton was, however, a more winnable seat. It was a predominantly working-class constituency stretching from Glasgow Cross to the boundary of the Shettleston Division. It was renowned for poverty and sectarian hatred among its Catholic and Protestant communities, whose employment was mainly in the engineering and textile works. In the run-up to the election, masses of street meetings were held and the Maxton camp had some room for optimism but things began to go badly when his election agent, George Eadie, was imprisoned (for reasons unknown) during the vital weeks of the campaign. John Muir took over but he could only devote his spare time as he was also standing as a candidate for the Maryhill Division. In the event the 'Coupon' election of 1918 brought few successes for the ILP. Lloyd George's promise to 'Hang the Kaiser' proved more popular with an hysterically jingoistic electorate than social reform. Maxton was defeated by his Coalition Liberal opponent, McCallum Scott (whom he later convinced to join the ILP), but there was victory for Neil Maclean at Govan and a near miss for

Wheatley in Shettleston. It would appear that the ILP did best in those constituencies where they had conducted the most anti-war activity and had been strongly involved in the 1915 rent strikes. Although the Unionists had won ten out of the fifteen Glasgow seats, the basis had been laid for an ILP breakthrough at the next opportunity.

The 1918 general election had been, in spite of encouraging electoral trends, interpreted as a failure by the Labour movement and this saw attention switched to the industrial arena again. At a conference in Glasgow on 27 and 28 December, the CWC called for the establishment of a thirty-hour week in industry as a means of preventing widespread unemployment following war demobilisation. The demand had the backing of the CWC, the ILP and the Scottish Trades Union Congress (STUC) as unemployment was already running at around eight per cent in the engineering industry but further discussion saw the demand watered down to a more achievable level of forty hours. The employers and government refused to accept the reduced hours and a strike ensued in co-operation with Belfast workers. On 27 January 1919 40,000 Glasgow workers came out on strike for a shorter working week. The next day the number had risen to 70,000 and the trend was upwards. Under pressure the government called a conference to settle the dispute but also (on the advice of Robert Munro, Secretary of State for Scotland, who was convinced that the strike was a Bolshevik uprising) took the precaution of despatching troops. The climax came when a large crowd gathered in George Square on 1 February to hear the government's decision on the conference. A riot occurred when the police baton-charged the crowd. Maxton at that moment was in the City Chambers and was probably saved from arrest because of this. Others were not so lucky. David Kirkwood was bludgeoned by the police and arrested on charges of instigating a riot, Emanuel Shinwell was given a five-month and Willie

Gallacher a three-month term of imprisonment for their part in the affair. However, ten other defendants, including Kirkwood, were found not guilty.

The arrests produced an electric situation in Glasgow. The government poured in 12,000 troops, 100 lorries and six tanks, placing the city under virtual military rule. The situation soon stabilised as the government adopted a more conciliatory line with the strikers. The conference was reconvened and the statutory regulation of wages and rents was retained for the immediate future. The strike fizzled out after this with a steady drift back to work. The 'revolution' was over and quiet flowed the Clyde. Politically, the failure of the Forty Hours Strike saw the revolutionary vanguard isolated as the move back to more orthodox political activity took place.

6

Whether the war years constituted a revolutionary opportunity for the left is still a lively debate among historians but, on the face of it, it would appear that the revolutionary potential of the Clydeside working class has been exaggerated. Firstly, outside of Maclean, who lacked a power base among the workers, none of the Labour leaders developed a class analysis of the war, nor did they seriously consider threatening the power and authority of the state. Secondly, it was the conduct of those running the war rather than the war itself which provoked so much anger and opposition within the Labour movement of the west of Scotland. From a class patriotic position Labour leaders attacked the inequality of sacrifice which government policies had created: fat profits for the Capitalists and financiers and poverty and hardship for the workers. Maxton's 1918 May Day manifesto makes this clear. It called for 'A Living Wage for All', the abolition of the food profiteer and 'Justice for our Soldiers and their dependants'. Thirdly, the massive demand the war made for fighting men meant that few families escaped personal loss of some kind. Undermining the war effort meant risking alienating the working class, something which few Labour leaders were prepared to do.

The caution of the ILP was matched by the reluctance of the revolutionary shop stewards to seriously politicise the workers during the struggles against the Munitions Act. The dilemma that active opposition to the war would seriously weaken the capacity of the state to wage war effectively was never really addressed by the CWC. Because of this, it was never able to utilise its industrial power to bring the war to an end. Most, when brought to trial on various charges connected with impeding the war effort, denied that this was their intention. At the trial of Gallacher and Muir a fellow worker was called to give evidence that they had opposed strikes and Gallacher added that he had 'no desire to impede production'. It was, therefore, perfectly understandable that Maclean, in his famous speech from the dock, should attack the CWC for their failure to transform the industrial struggle into an all-out political struggle against the war. Among the far left, then, it was only Maclean who adopted a revolutionary class position and, as was mentioned above, he lacked mass support.

Although the First World War did not create a revolutionary situation on Clydeside in the Marxist sense, this should not blind us to the important political and social changes it generated. There occurred fundamental shifts in the balance of power in society. The free market in housing rents was destroyed and the state was forced to co-operate with the trade unions in running the economy. The hegemony of the Liberal Party in Scotland was broken by leaders like Maxton and Wheatley and a host of activists. The personal standing of those who had taken part in the peace movement was raised immensely. The names of Dollan, Johnston, Maxton and Wheatley would come to dominate discussion on the inter-war Labour movement in Scotland and elsewhere. The political direction of the Labour movement in the west of Scotland was clearly mapped. The main beneficiaries of the wartime struggles were the ILP and not Maclean or the CWC. The ILP's success lay in the fact that it recognised the limits of working-class protest more clearly than any of its left-wing rivals. Therefore, it was able to translate this into a policy which accurately reflected the alternative political economy of the Glasgow working class. Two years after the disappointment of the 1918 general election the ILP would win forty-five seats in the municipal elections, serving notice that the next election would be the stuff of high political drama. Maxton and the rest of the Glasgow ILP were ready to step onto the stage of national politics.

3 Westminster

1

Maxton's disappointment at failing to win a parliamentary seat in the 1918 General Election was tempered somewhat by his appointment in early 1919 as Scottish organiser of the ILP at a salary of £5 a week and by his election to the Executive of the Labour Party. With a regular source of income, Maxton contemplated marriage. He had become engaged to an engineer's daughter, Sissie McCallum, while in Duke Street Prison. They had met when Maxton was at Haghill Public School. Under Maxton's influence Sissie joined the Scottish Socialist Teachers' Society, which meant there was a political, as well as a physical, attraction and compatibility in the relationship. In spite of the fact that the bride's parents disapproved of the marriage and in spite of Maxton's atheism, the marriage took place on 24 July 1919 in Glasgow's Episcopalian Christ's Church. Respectability, it seems, was more important than conviction.

This was the beginning of what was reputed to be the happiest time of Maxton's life but it did not last long. Sissie Maxton was not a physically strong woman – a bout of rheumatic fever had left her with a weak heart – and her condition was not improved by their council home in Garngad, one of Glasgow's poorest areas. To be near his sickly wife, Maxton resigned his post as Scottish organiser and became full-time secretary of the Glasgow ILP Federation in 1920. The following year a son, James, was born. However, the child was seriously ill for a year and in need of constant attention. Nursing almost night and day drained the life from the mother and, as the child grew in strength, she grew weaker and fell dangerously ill herself. A few days later she died. The effect of Sissie's death on Maxton was profound and something from which he never recovered. All that saved him from total collapse was his love for his son and his political work, something which his brother John had to take over for six months while Maxton recovered. Indeed, his relationship with his son was extremely close. It was said that they were more like friends than father and son, sharing their joys and sorrows in intimate companionship. Young James joined the ILP when older and remained in it until his untimely death from a heart attack in the late 1950s. This put an end to what was an exceptional medical career. He was Scotland's youngest medical officer.

At the time of his wife's death, Maxton was an elected member of the Glasgow Education Authority (GEA) for Shettleston and Bridgeton. This was quite an achievement in circumstances where the electorate was polarised on religious grounds. Maxton was able to win votes from Catholics and Protestants alike. His work in the GEA proved to be as important in shaping his longer-term ideological development as his involvement with the CWC and other left-wing bodies. At the GEA he concerned himself with a wide spectrum of social issues manifest in conditions of deepening economic depression in the city. With demobilisation and the end of the immediate post-war restocking boom, the Scottish economy entered a period of sustained depression lasting almost twenty years. In conditions of economic slump, the authorities, under pressure from central government, were making cuts in education and the social services. Maxton and his ILP colleagues on the GEA fought hard to modify the cost-cutting policies of the local authority.

The range of issues for which Maxton fought included, amongst other things, the provision of free books in schools, increases in school bursaries, free tuition at evening school for needy students and improved conditions and salaries for teachers. However, the major concern for the ILP was the feeding and clothing of necessitous children. The Education (Scotland) Act of 1918 permitted the local authorities to provide for the needy and Maxton, at a meeting of the GEA on 3 November 1921, moved a resolution demanding that the Act be carried out in full. He moved that 'in view of the general distress all education authorities ought to provide three meals daily – including Sundays – for all children in need'. Throughout this period Maxton was also in touch with the Unemployed Committees in Glasgow and pressurised the authorities to maintain at least minimal provisions in hostels and feeding centres.

2

Maxton's time on the GEA brought him into conflict with the Scottish churches. The latter condemned him for supporting the abolition of the shorter catechism in religious instruction in schools. The repercussions of that opposition were felt in the next round of elections for the GEA. To halt what they saw as the creeping secularisation of education the churches entered the election and Labour lost four seats on the authority. In March 1922 Maxton himself was only narrowly re-elected. He attacked the Protestant churches for Labour's poor showing, declaring 'It is the Protestant churches. . . which will suffer in the days to come. . . It is not good business. . . for the Protestant churches to stand blatantly as the enemies of the working class even when the attack is made behind the mask of religion.'[5]

Maxton returned to the assault on Protestant churches when in 1925 he opposed in the Commons the Church of Scotland receiving financial support from the state as the established church, on the grounds that it discriminated against other denominations and religions. Again in that year he criticised the attempts by the established church and the United Free Church (UFC) to obtain an amendment to the 1918 Education Act which would prevent Protestant taxes being used to finance Catholic education. Maxton defended the right of Catholics to be educated in the 'faith of their fathers' and wrote off the Church of Scotland as a 'narrow-minded and intolerant sect'.

Attacks on the Protestant churches led some contemporaries to brand Maxton a crypto-Catholic. It was true that in Bridgeton the sectarian gangs tended if Catholic to be pro-Maxton and if Protestant anti-Maxton. It was also well-known that Maxton was a supporter of Glasgow Celtic Football Club, which had strong links with the Catholic priesthood and Irish Republicans, and that he received proportionately more votes from Catholics than non-Catholics. The Catholic Irish connection was a political necessity. Given the denominational structure of the Bridgeton electorate, no one could hope to be elected without Catholic support. Indeed, Maxton won enthusiastic support from Catholics and endorsement from the Catholic Church at the 1922 General Election and subsequent elections but the support was given on a conditional basis. The price was silence on social issues such as abortion, birth control and segregated denominational schooling; indeed, anything calculated to harm the interests of the church.

On more than one occasion Maxton had to act against ILP policy on education and birth control. During the late 1920s and early 1930s, Maxton repeatedly ignored ILP policy on secular education and supported the continuation of religious instruction in schools. In 1930-1 Maxton disillusioned some of his left-wing friends by failing to defend Sir Charles Trevelyan's Education Bill, which proposed raising the school leaving age to fifteen, allowing it to be savaged by Catholic MPs demanding more money for Catholic education. Maxton's reply to his critics was that, although he favoured secular education, he did not wish to 'divide the working class by religious antagonism'. Similarly, his views on birth control were unconvincing. Rather than recognise the liberating potential birth control held for women, allowing them to play an active part in society and the Labour movement, Maxton advocated the 'intelligent control of the appetites and desires'. His twentieth-century malthusianism was attacked by Dora Russell, wife of Bertrand, who rightly concluded that 'The shadow of threatened religious opposition blinds many Scottish members' to the advantages of birth control. Losing the Catholic vote was too great a fear for Maxton to renounce sectarian alliances, which in practice meant that he was prepared to deliberately obfuscate whole areas of Socialist debate concerning the family and gender relationships. However, such views were not simply opportunistic . Maxton was fairly conventional when it came to questions surrounding the sexual division of labour and relationships between the sexes. His first marriage operated on the basis of the notion of the male as breadwinner and the female as housekeeper and mother, and, in spite of his reputed powers of attraction to women, Maxton never allowed this to develop beyond friendship. As Lord Beaverbrook, the newspaper magnate, said when speaking of Jenny Lee: 'She is Maxton's darling. I mean his political darling, for Jim Maxton has no darlings in the sexual sense, poor fellow.'

3

The 1922 General Election proved a spectacular success for Labour, particularly in Glasgow where they won ten out of the fifteen parliamentary constituencies. The shift to the left among the Glasgow electorate has been the subject of extensive analysis but it would appear to be the result of four factors – the extension of the franchise, the ending of Irish Home Rule as a vital electoral issue, housing and unemployment.

The election was fought against a backdrop of mass unemployment and social distress. The post-war promise of Lloyd George of a 'land fit for heroes' had a hollow ring to it as the government's deflationary policies led to cuts in social spending and directly contributed to unemployment. The level of unemployment in Scotland rose to twenty per cent with the heavy capital goods industries like coal, iron and steel and shipbuilding in rapid decline. Mass unemployment led to sharpening of economic discontent which, since the extension of the franchise, was better able to make its presence felt in the political arena. After February 1918 most of the complicated electoral registration procedures and franchise anomalies were abolished. Women over the age of thirty were enfranchised, as were lodgers and grown up children living at home. The legislation resulted in a more working-class electorate and disturbed the traditional balance of power – something with which the disunited Liberal Party could not cope. Women especially were inclined to vote Labour. *Forward* noted that in the election 'a majority of women. . . voted Labour' and that 'women's meetings were marked by a religious fervour for social reform and justice'. Ex-servicemen were also more likely to vote Labour, as were many middle-class people for the first time. The *Catholic Observer* advised its readers to vote Labour as it had proved the most sympathetic of all the political parties to providing out of the rates for Catholic education. The Catholic press had, however, no real choice, since, with the signing of the Irish Treaty in 1921, Partition removed the issue of Home Rule from the political agenda for decades to come. After 1921 the Liberals had little to offer the Irish Catholics, and, rather than see them move in the direction of the atheistic Communist Party of Great Britain (CPGB), the Catholic Church advised its communicants to vote Labour as the lesser of two evils. Finally, the shrewdness with which Labour exploited the discontent over housing conditions also bore fruit. The Rent Restrictions Act of 1915 was accredited to its efforts. A House of Lords' judgement in a test case under the act sponsored by the Labour Party immediately prior to the General Election awarded a refund to the tenants from the landlords for past paid rent. While other parties distanced themselves from the award, Labour produced a handbill declaring: 'If you want your rent returned you must vote Labour'. The idea of a rent rebate had tremendous electoral appeal to the Glasgow workers, most of whom lived in rented accommodation. Added to these immediate factors were, of course, the longer-term effects of the political radicalisation of large parts of the working class during the war years.

It was these factors which provided the context for Labour's electoral breakthrough in Glasgow and it was only to be expected that Maxton, as the most popular figure in city politics, would be part of the triumph. Indeed, his victory was almost a foregone conclusion, as in the municipal elections prior to November 1922 three Labour candidates were elected in Bridgeton in preference to three moderates. Maxton won by a 7,692 majority over his old rival McCallum Scott. From this point onwards until his death in 1946, Maxton had an unbreakable hold over the constituency. In 1935 he recorded the lowest ever expenditure in a General Election when his campaign costs totalled a mere £54. Maxton's immense popularity with the people of Bridgeton gave rise to the saying 'that they didn't count his votes only weighed them.'

The sweeping victory of November 1922 generated an enthusiasm in Glasgow which bordered on the millenial. Mass meetings to celebrate the triumph were held all over the city. On Sunday, 20 November at St Andrew's Hall a service of dedication was held at which the audience sang the 124th Psalm – 'Had not the Lord been on our side'. The climax to the celebrations was the rousing send-off the Clydeside MPs received at St Enoch's station. Around 250,000 people packed the surrounding streets to see Maxton and the others off to London. The scene was almost biblical The crowd sang some old Scots songs and *Jerusalem*, climaxing with the *Red Flag* and the *Internationale*. Maxton addressed the seething throng of people, warning the government that it could expect nothing from them but implacable opposition. In a mock-rephrasing of an old hymn Maxton ridiculed the Conservative leader's slogan – 'peace and tranquility' – musing thus:

> Bonar [Law], seek not yet repose,
> Cast the dream of rest away;
> Thou art in the midst of foes,
> Watch and Pray.

David Kirkwood assured the workers that, when they returned, the railways would belong to them. The so-called 'wild men' were on their way, burning with indignation at the social evils around them and missionary in their zeal to correct them. However, as they would find, it would take more than rhetoric.

4

The arrival of the 'Clydesiders' proved something of a London sensation. In the Commons and in the smart London society they shocked their political opponents by refusing to socialise with them and neither did they accept social invitations from rich Labour members. Maxton, along with Rev Campbell Stephen, MP for Calmachie, and George Buchanan, trades unionist and MP for Gorbals, lived a rather solitary existence, firstly in Pimlico and later in Battersea. Their main entertainment was long fireside chats and, in Maxton's case, copious supplies of coffee and cigarettes. None of the three touched alcohol, which was not unusual among Scottish Labour leaders; temperance had long been a distinguishing feature of the Scottish Labour movement. Writing in *Forward* in June 1918, Maxton stated that Labour's aim was for the 'total prohibition of the liquor trade'. As such, one of the Clydesiders' first acts in parliament was to support prohibition in the form of Labour MP for Dundee Edwin Scrymgeour's Liquor Traffic Control Bill. The Bill contained draconian measures such as the immediate closure of all public houses, five years' imprisonment for trafficking in liquor and so on. It failed, however, to get a second reading and was defeated by 236 votes to 14.

Another of the Glasgow MPs' first actions was to play an important part in the election of Ramsay MacDonald as leader of the Labour Party. MacDonald's stand against the war, although never emphatically oppositional, was sufficient to endear him to many in the Clydeside group, particularly Kirkwood and Shinwell. According to Beatrice Webb in *Diaries* (1952), the 'ILP members reinforced by the Scottish group of extremists, had determined to gvie. . . pride of place to their chief man [MacDonald]'. It was the votes of the Clydesiders which swung a narrow election margin MacDonald's way. Maxton's role in this affair is, however, open to some controversy. John Scanlon in *The Decline and Fall of the Labour Party* (1932) claims that Maxton assured him that the Clydeside group, including himself, were 'all voting for Mac-Donald' and this is supported by John McNair in *James Maxton: The Beloved Rebel* (1955). However, both Iain McLean in *The Legend of Red Clydeside* (1983) and David Marquand in *Ramsay MacDonald* (1977) have argued to the contrary, claiming that Maxton opposed MacDonald, and, according to the latter, proposed John Wheatley instead. Wheatley's anonymity made him an unlikely leader and he was on record as being a committed MacDonald man. The only realistic alternatives to the latter were J. R. Clynes and J. H. Thomas, both disliked by Maxton, particularly Clynes. Therefore, while Maxton at a meeting of ILP MPs may have voiced opposition to MacDonald, when it came to the full meeting of the Parliamentary Labour Party (PLP) he fell in line with the other Clydesiders and voted for MacDonald. There was also nothing in Maxton's subsequent actions which showed that he harboured any antagonism to MacDonald. However, in the following year the latter would have less to thank the Maxton group for.

5

Much of Maxton's time in the Commons was spent campaigning for improved welfare benefits to assist the poor and the aged. To this end his maiden speech was delivered on 8 December 1922 against existing unemployment legislation, especially the 'not genuinely seeking work' clause and the low level of benefits. With the Commons controlled by the Tories and with no prospect of a General Election before 1926 or 1927, little success was anticipated or achieved. This led Maxton and some of his close associates to the opinion that these issues were in need of greater publicity and more urgency. The PLP under the leadership of MacDonald was too responsible and, because of this, unwilling to engage in confrontational politics with the Baldwin govern-ment. The Maxton group felt that government had to be relentlessly confronted and an issue found which would create a political storm and scandalise the government into action on behalf of the unemployed. Therefore, it was a deliberately agreed tactic to create some sort of scene in the Commons but when the opportunity arose it came unexpectedly in a debate on 27 June 1923 on the Scottish Health Board Estimates.

As part of the government's deflationary strategy, health grants to local authorities had been cut at a time when it was reported that the incidence of tuberculosis had increased by eleven per cent. Clearly with the memory of his son's illness and his wife's recent death at the forefront of his mind, Maxton, shaking with emotion, rose to deliver one of the most powerful speeches of his career. In front of a packed House he condemned the cuts, claiming that the only outcome would be the death of children. He also criticised the withdrawal in 1922 of the Board of Health's financial support to local authorities to provide hospital accommodation to children suffering from measles and whooping cough. The removal of the facilities, Maxton charged, meant that 'In the interests of economy the MPs [who approved the Board's action] condemned hundreds of children to death and I call it murder. I call the men who introduced the policy murderers. I call the men who walked into the lobby in support of that policy murderers. They have on their hands the blood of infants – the blood of infants.' When Sir Frederick Banbury, Conservative, objected, Maxton called him the 'worst murderer' of all. On an order from the Speaker of the House to withdraw his remark, Maxton refused. He stood his ground for half-an-hour until, overcome by physical exhaustion, he sat down, only for his place to be taken by Wheately, who repeated the charge, then Stephen and, finally, Buchanan. After a Commons vote in which the whole of the Labour front bench abstained, MacDonald reputedly seething with anger, the four MPs were suspended.

Although their actions outraged the leadership of the PLP, the suspended MPs received enthusiastic support from within the Labour movement. Tom Johnston, who acted as one of the tellers for the Maxton group in the Commons vote, urged Maxton not to apologise for his remark. Johnston's sentiments were shared by the Executive of the Scottish ILP, Glasgow ILP Federation and the GTC, all of whom sent telegrams of support. However, the editor of the leading ILP journal, *New Leader*, H. N. Brailsford dismissed the protest as a cheap stunt which had not only served to 'discredit Parliament itself' but also 'weakened the prestige of Mr MacDonald'. Taking up where the *New Leader* left off, the Conference Arrangements Committee refused to allow on the agenda of the July 1923 Labour Party conference a resolution dealing with the suspension of Maxton and the others. MacDonald in a short speech asked conference to let the PLP deal with the matter. Following this, Maxton tried to address conference but was shouted down and a motion, moved by J. T. Brownlie of the Amalgamated Engineering Union, calling for the next business was carried by a massive majority. After more uproar Maxton was finally allowed to speak. The intervention was a bit of an anti-climax. All Maxton wished to say was that he associated himself 'absolutely with the statement made by the leader'.

Maxton's conciliatory gesture was made in the full knowledge that MacDonald was working behind the scenes to get him and the other suspended MPs reinstated. Correspondence between the two men contained in Maxton's personal papers demonstrates that Maxton was using the incident to make as much political capital as he could. Time and time again, MacDonald tried to arrange a meeting with Maxton to discuss the situation but he refused. MacDonald also informed him that it was Baldwin's intransigency and not his own which was the major stumbling block to reinstatement.

Failure to make progress saw MacDonald becoming more exasperated. Maxton and the other suspended MPs issued a public statement declaring that on 30 July they would force their way into the Commons and claim their right to represent their constituents. The attempt was unsuccessful and prompted a scathing rebuke from MacDonald. The Labour leader argued that the attempt had merely succeeded in hindering his arrangement to get them reinstated – which was to be not later than 2 August. Maxton was warned about his future conduct. MacDonald said that, although he was prepared to tolerate a wide variety of opinions, 'a limit has to be observed, and I draw it at the point when I am convinced that individuality begins to express itself as a separate entity. . . as an independent, self-satisfied centre of agitation'. Maxton apologised and on 31 July he was, with the assistance of Baldwin, back in the Commons along with the others.

6

1923 also saw Maxton making his mark in international affairs. In late February and early March, along with Kirkwood, Stephen and Wheatley, he visited the Ruhr to assess the impact of the French occupation on the standard of living of the German working class and international relations. While in Germany they canvassed a wide spectrum of opinion including the British Consul General for the Rhineland, the British Vice-Consul for Essen, a director of Krupps, the executive of the Ruhr miners' union, and the French Commander-in-Chief. From their investigation the Maxton group drew two conclusions; firstly, that, in spite of French occupation, German workers enjoyed a higher material condition of life than workers in the west of Scotland and could hardly be described, as the NAC of the ILP had done, as the 'serfs of a foreign taskmaster'; and, secondly, that the coalfields of the Ruhr and Lorraine should be treated as one and placed under international control. Actually, Maxton had been convinced of the first conclusion for some time. While holidaying with his wife he had written to his sister, Annie, from Salzburg about his stay in Munich. He claimed that he had 'to look closely to see the signs of poverty and suffering in Germany'. Thus, in this respect, his mind was already made up on the issue before he left for the Ruhr in 1923.

The Maxton group also advocated placing the coalfields of the Ruhr and Lorraine under the control of a board of international directors drawn from France, Germany, Britain, Belgium and Italy. The dividends from the coal sales were to be divided proportionately as war reparations with guarantees of good wages for the miners. Germany's gain would be the removal of foreign troops from her soil. Additionally, the allies, by fixing a reasonable figure as reparations, would give the German government the incentive to work harmoniously with them to liquidate the country's war debt. The dividends to the allies would be increased by their saving on military expenditure. France would have her national safety guaranteed by international control of German war materials. Britain would be safeguarded against the overwhelming advantages in world markets which a monopoly of the Ruhr and Lorraine coal would give France. Italy and Belgium would gain in status by sharing in the control of the coalfields. The whole world would benefit by the greater sense of security and common interest created by such a settlement.

The view that the material standard of the German working class had not suffered as a result of the French occupation of the Ruhr was attacked by the *New Leader*. Brailsford pointed out that the level of real wages in the Ruhr had fallen by as much as two-thirds since the French occupation and that Maxton's comparison with Glasgow was a false one. Housing conditions were worse in Glasgow than the Rhur, but then they were inferior to most English cities as well. Brailsford's position may have been factually sound, but he failed to realise that the Maxton group were using their report to shift the focus of the ILP away from its traditional interest in foreign affairs to almost exclusive interest in domestic issues. Along with Wheatley, Maxton took the view that foreign policy held little interest for Clydeside workers: what mattered to the working class was action on economic and social questions. The idea that the treatment of one set of foreign nationals by another could influence the outcome of a general election had died with Gladstone in the nineteenth century. The move towards domestic policy was designed to end the influence of radical Liberalism, with its internationalist outlook, and replace it with a more Socialist, if somewhat narrowly nationalist, emphasis in the ILP.

Maxton had no theory of foreign affairs, indeed, he had no need for one. His attitudes were somewhat parochial at this time. Early in 1920 he had opposed the decision of the Scottish Divisional Council of the ILP to support affiliation to the Bolshevik Third International. Four years later he attacked the Baldwin government for making a £120 million loan to Greece, suggesting that the money could have been better invested 'in the brawn and muscle and brain of a decent race in this great Britain of ours'. In 1925, in a debate on foreign manufactures, Tory lack of patriotism was roasted by Maxton for placing an order for motor ships in Germany when it could have been placed on the Clyde. Maxton's nationalist sympathies were also expressed in his rhetoric. He was fond of using patriotic phrases such as 'our country', 'my country', and 'disgrace to the British way of life' which, although interpretable in class patriotic terms, were quite at odds with a Socialist internationalist perspective. It was only towards the end of the 1920s that his attitudes to overseas aid and narrow nationalism changed – something which can be put down to his acceptance of Lenin's theory of imperialism.

7

Towards the end of 1923 the Conservatives decided to call an election on the question of tariff reform. The threatened introduction of protectionism had the effect of uniting the Liberals behind Asquith's leadership under the banner of free trade. Labour too was inclined towards the support of free trade, showing that its affinity with certain important aspects of radical Liberalism still existed. The election results left no party with a clear majority: Labour won 191 seats, Liberals 158 and the Conservatives 258. Although the latter was clearly the largest party, the vote was interpreted as a rebuff to protectionism. The two parties of free trade co-operated with each other and a deal was struck which put Labour in office as the larger of the two. The election had conclusively proved that Labour was the most serious political challenger to the dominance of the Conservatives.

The December election saw the return of Maxton to the

Commons and an increased Labour vote, although a note of personal tragedy was struck when Maxton's mother died during the election campaign. Prior to the establishment of the Labour government Maxton had spoken out against taking power for power's sake and of forming a government dependent on survival on 'some party whose basis was not Socialistic'. A Labour government relying on Liberal support for its survival, argued Maxton, inevitably meant a severe watering-down of the party's manifesto. MacDonald and the other party leaders were disinclined to accept Maxton's views as they felt that government offered Labour the opportunity to rebut Churchill's criticism that it was incapable of government. But as events were to prove the price was high: the Labour government would be short-lived, disintegrating under the onslaught of political and media pressure with little constructive legislation to show for its time in office.

4 The first Labour government

1

Maxton, like other Clydesiders, was never quite at ease in London. He had a strong sense of Scottishness and this led to chronic bouts of homesickness. However, his attachment to his native land was not simply emotional; Maxton was strongly committed to the idea of Home Rule for Scotland. This was an early political demand of the modern Labour movement in Scotland and was part of its shared ethos with popular Liberalism. The demand became more urgent following the experiences of the war years and the optimism created by the immediate post-war economic boom, which seemed to provide for self-government on a sound and prosperous economic foundation. It was as a response to the new mood of nationalist fervour that Roland Muirhead, a wealthy businessman, set up the Scottish Home Rule Association (SHRA) in 1918. Maxton was a member from the outset and did much to popularise the idea of self-government among the Scottish workers. Although it was non-party in intention, the SHRA soon attracted widespread support from the Scottish Labour movement. At the peak of its influence (1922-4) membership included fifty political organisations, sixty co-operative societies, 150 trades unions and twenty-nine Labour MPs. Few Labourites paid any attention to a ruling from the Scottish Council of the Labour Party that Labour members should not join the SHRA and instead work for Home Rule exclusively through their own party. Johnston and Maxton, in direct breach of party policy, addressed several rallies under the auspices of the SHRA at Eldersie – the birthplace of William Wallace. One of his speeches at Eldersie was published by the SHRA under the title of *James Maxton and Scotland*

Like a number of the leading figures in the Scottish Labour movement, Maxton was convinced that the Scottish working class was more politically conscious than its English counterpart. Home Rule for Scotland would mean that Socialism could be achieved more rapidly in the north than if the Scots remained fully integrated into the Westminster system. The culmination of this movement was the introduction in the Commons in 1924 of George Buchanan's Government of Scotland Bill, which provided for an independent Scotland within a federal Britain. Speaking at a rally in Glasgow in support of the Bill, Maxton declared that 'He would ask for no greater task in life than to make the English-ridden, capitalist-ridden, landowner-ridden Scotland into a free Scottish Socialist Commonwealth. . . with Scottish brains and courage. . . we could do more in five years in a Scottish Parliament than would be produced by 25 or 30 years' heartbreaking work in the British House of Commons'.[6] In spite of having the support of all the Scottish Labour MPs, Buchanan's Bill did not enjoy government backing. MacDonald avoided making any commitment to Home Rule and the Tories were allowed to talk it out. Maxton continued to reaffirm his support for self-government for Scotland throughout the 1920s, as did the Labour Party, but the immediacy and the impact Home Rule had had in the heady political atmosphere of the immediate post-war years was never recaptured. Part of the reason for this lay with the declining fortunes of the Scottish economy, and part lay with the changing character and structure of Scottish trades unionism. Following the end of the post-war restocking boom, the heavy capital goods industries like coal, shipbuilding and iron and steel went into rapid decline. The government's deflationary policy accelerated this process with the result that in the 1920s unemployment in Scotland averaged around fourteen per cent; 2.6 per cent higher than the UK average, with periods of unemployment experienced by as much as three-fifths of the working population. Unemployment, of course, was much higher in specific industries. For example, on Clydeside the numbers employed in shipbuilding had fallen by fifty per cent, or from 100,000 to 50,000 in the years 1920-5, and in mining and metals the numbers employed fell between 1921 and 1931 by twenty-three and eighteen per cent respectively. The downturn in the economy initiated new departures within the trades union movement which militated against Home Rule sentiment. Trades unions sought to increase their strength by amalgamations and mergers; a process which was accelerated by the existence of national wage-bargaining structures and industrial unionism. By 1925 three out of five Scottish trades unionists were members of British unions and those who maintained a form of autonomy, like the miners, were linked to English unions by the creation of federal structures. From 1923 onwards the STUC ceased to debate the issue of Home Rule. It seemed to many in the Labour movement, including Maxton, that such changes meant that the best hope in the meantime for Scotland and the working class lay with the Labour government. But in this they were to be sorely disappointed.

2

The desire of MacDonald to project a moderate and respectable image to the middle classes ensured that his Cabinet would be dominated by the centre-right but, as a sop to the left, John Wheatley and Fred Jowett were included, the former as Minister of Health. Some of the most talented of the Clydeside MPs were excluded. Maxton was not forgiven for the 'murderers' incident but, in any case, his image was too wild. Tom Johnston was not considered as he had embarrassed MacDonald in 1923 by exposing the financial scandal of the Sudan cotton-growing syndicate which involved Asquith's son. Both Johnston and Maxton were angry at their omission – Johnston more than Maxton. What hurt them most was the gossip circulating round Westminster which suggested that exclusion was made on intellectual and not on tactical grounds: 'Because he [MacDonald] thinks we haven't got the brains,' complained Maxton.

Maxton's omission did not make him ill-disposed towards the new government. He had previously expressed opposition towards the establishment of a minority Labour government but, once in power, he felt that there was no mileage to be gained from being too critical of it. Indeed, Maxton said in 1924 that Labour in office had 'accomplished wonders' and that MacDonald's Cabinet was 'a good, sound representative of every interest in the Labour movement'. Thus, for all his supposed wild image, Maxton was still a loyal member of the PLP and said little publicly to embarrass the government. His loyalty was recognised in his membership of Labour's parliamentary committee, whose role was to deal with internal administration and to act as a conduit between government and party. It also had responsibility for the selection of party representatives to serve on the Common's select and standing committees.

His worth to the MacDonald government was shown in the notorious J. R. Campbell case which ultimately led to the fall of the government. Campbell was a leading member of the CPGB and editor of the *Workers' Weekly*. On 25 July 1924 the newspaper published an article asking soldiers not to turn their guns on workers in class or civil war. On 6 August, the day on which the Anglo/Soviet trade agreements were being negotiated, the Tories raised the question of the article in the Commons. The Attorney General, Sir Patrick Hastings, announced that the government intended to prosecute Campbell under the 1795

Incitement to Mutiny Act. The decision was strongly criticised from the Labour benches. Maxton argued that the article was merely a request for troops not to be used in industrial disputes and that this was hardly out of step with Labour Party policy. Maxton's attitude corresponded with that of the government and the seemingly inconsequential issue was dropped on 13 August.

As far as Labour was concerned, that put an end to the matter. However, when the summer recess was over the Tories returned to the offensive and forced the government to set aside time for a special debate on 8 October. In the meantime Hastings consulted Maxton about Campbell and was informed of the latter's impressive war record and the fact that he was only acting editor. Campbell had no power to prevent the publication of the article as this was decided for him by the CPGB's politbureau. Hastings relayed this information to the Commons during the debate but it made little impression on the Tories and their Liberal allies and the vote went against Labour. Since MacDonald had elevated the issue to a question of no confidence in the government he had no option but to resign and call a General Election.

The election was marked by the so-called Zinoviev letter; a communication purportedly written by the president of Cominform, Zinoviev, to Arthur McManus, the Chairman of the CPGB. The letter called for increased pressure on the Labour government to conclude the trade agreements with the USSR. It also urged British Communists to step up propaganda among the working class, the army and the navy to overthrow Capitalism. Four days before the election the letter was published in the *Daily Mail* under the heading 'Communist plots in Britain'. MacDonald's handling of the affair was particularly inept and seemed to give credence to the authenticity of the document. Labour was depicted by its opponents as a tool of Bolshevik foreign policy and there is little doubt that this was a major factor in their defeat at the election. The Zinoviev letter augmented the Conservative vote by adding to it ex-Liberals and the normally apathetic.

Labour was reduced to 151 seats in the new parliament although it had increased its share of the poll, mainly at the expense of the Liberals. When the PLP reconvened, MacDonald was re-elected party leader, although not before he came in for some savage criticism over his handling of the Zinoviev letter and the tameness of the Labour government when in office. Maxton was foremost among the critics. He moved George Lansbury as leader but the proposal only received five votes. Robert Smillie, the highly respected veteran miners' leader, argued that it would be unfair to dismiss MacDonald on the morning of defeat and this view was shared by the majority of the PLP. Maxton accepted the decision and did not seek to cause MacDonald further embarrassment over the Zinoviev affair. As a member of a party investigative committee, which also included J. H. Thomas and William Graham, Maxton exonerated Mac-Donald of any blame. At the 1925 ILP Conference he asked the delegates not to probe too deeply into the incident but at the same time he accused the Conservatives of being behind the affair.

Although he did not wish to upset MacDonald more than was necessary, there were clear signs that Maxton was unhappy, not only with the performance of the Labour government, but also with the general political direction of Labour. During the Campbell case, John Scanlon disclosed to him that the prosecution of the former might wreck the Labour government. Maxton replied: 'the sooner they are out of office the better, as every day they were in, led us further from Socialism'. The first Labour government had been a disappointment to all but its staunchest supporters. The only legislative success was Wheatley's Housing Act and in foreign affairs the removal of French troops from the Ruhr. With the re-election of MacDonald as leader, what were private thoughts became increasingly public as Maxton began to mouth his dissatisfaction with the gradualism of the Labour Party. With Lansbury and Wheatley, he organised a left-wing section of the PLP determined to pursue the principles and policies of the Labour Party, even if it meant going against the leadership. In order to ensure the maximum amount of freedom for political manoeuvre, Maxton refused to sit on the Executive of the PLP. This meant he could not be compromised by any form of collective responsibility resulting from his membership of the PLP Executive.

3

By now, Maxton was perhaps the most popular member of the ILP and the leading spokesman of the left in Britain. This drew him into conflict with the Chairman of the ILP, Clifford Allen. What separated the men at a social level was Maxton's 'difficulty in extending his spontaneous friendship' towards 'frigid, middle class intellectuals', one of whom he considered Allen to be.[7] At a political level, it was Maxton's support for no compensation in the event of land nationalisation at the 1925 Labour Party Conference which strained relations between them to breaking point. Allen was in favour of compensation and, along with Maxton, had been a member of the ILP Commission on Compensation which had reported in favour of this policy. This was further ratified by the York ILP Conference in April 1924. Maxton disregarded the decision of conference and cast his vote at the Labour Party Conference in September against compensation. The climax was reached in October 1925 when, at a meeting of the NAC, Maxton proposed that MacDonald be relieved of the editorship of the *Socialist Review*. This was accepted by the NAC and Allen immediately resigned. Fred Jowett acted as temporary Chairman until Maxton's election, by a majority of over 500 votes, at the 1926 ILP Conference. Maxton held this position until 1931 and, after a three year respite, again from 1934-9.

The official reason for Allen's resignation was ill-health but it is clear from his subsequent letter to Maxton that it was his behaviour at the Labour Party's Liverpool Conference which made the decision for Allen. He wrote, complaining bitterly:

> Your POLITICAL actions at Liverpool were perhaps the most decisive factor in making me do what I did. . . When I saw the future Chairman of the party revealing that he considered himself entitled to pledge the Party to Land Nationalisation without compensation in flagrant defiance of the recorded decision of the Annual Conference at York, I realised that the future of the party was destroyed. . . I can't work with that kind of political irresponsibility.[8]

Maxton's high-handedness in casting his vote against agreed party policy was, however, upheld by the NAC. His election to the party chairmanship by an overwhelming majority showed how out of touch Allen was with the rank and file of the ILP. Allen's desire to move closer to the MacDonald leadership was at odds with the wishes of the membership and with the general left turn in the Labour movement. This was however to prove only temporarily to Maxton's advantage and would disappear as opposition to his more militant policies became more vociferous in the late 1920s and early 1930s. At that time the rank and file, following the disappointment of the first Labour government, were in a militant mood after the success of 'Red Friday'. On 30 June 1925 the coal-owners announced cuts in wages and a lengthening of the working day. The miners refused to accept the owners' terms and were supported in this by the TUC. The TUC announced that, in the event of a strike breaking out in the coal industry, it would impose an embargo on the shipment of coal and would be prepared to call a sympathetic General Strike in support of the miners. This threat forced the owners and the government to back down and accede to the miners' demands while yet another commission investigated the condition of the coal industry. Maxton symbolised this new fighting mood.

Coming from Glasgow and having taken part in the industrial and political struggles of the war years, Maxton did not subscribe to the traditional separate spheres policy of the ILP. As early as September 1924, in a speech delivered in Dundee, he put forward the need for the trades union movement to supplement political action with industrial, extra-parliamentary forms of protest. During the Glasgow rent strikes of March 1924 Maxton actually warned the Labour front bench in the Commons that he would lead the tenants onto the streets of Glasgow if the government refused to defend them against the landlords. It was this policy of confrontation, and not the cautious gradualism of Allen, which was at one with the mood of the Labour movement in the run up to the General Strike of 1926.

4

Maxton also fought for and advocated the maximum unity in the Labour movement. At the Scottish ILP Conference in January 1925 Maxton moved a resolution favouring the affiliation of the CPGB to the Labour Party. The resolution was defeated by 127 votes to 86, with Patrick Dollan the main opponent of affiliation. This was the beginning of a rift in the Scottish ILP which eventually would undermine Maxton's power base in Scotland. But, undaunted by defeat in Glasgow, Maxton attended a meeting convened in May by the Communist paper, the *Sunday Worker*, to set up a united left-wing movement in the struggle against Capitalism. Besides leading Communists, among those attending were important trades unionists such as A. B. Swales, President of the TUC, and A. A. Purcell, Vice-President of the TUC, as well as some ILP MPs. Although nothing was formally agreed, an unofficial National Left Wing Movement was launched. Part of its policy was affiliation and Maxton spoke for this at the Labour Party Conference, only to be defeated by a massive majority. The CPGB was a proscribed organisation, although this did not stop it co-operating from time to time with those Labourites grouped around the *Sunday Worker* and the left-wing movement. The movement might have been more successful had not CPGB leaders like Palme Dutt persisted in carrying out repeated attacks on sympathetic figures like Maxton.

Maxton was by no means a Bolshevik in his political outlook; he remained committed to the parliamentary road to Socialism. In his pamphlet, *Twenty Points for Socialism* (1925), he argued that Socialism could only come about through the 'peaceful and orderly transformation of society' and not, as the CPGB preached, by 'violent and catastrophic revolution'. In spite of fundamental disagreements with Communist philosophy, Maxton still felt that the CPGB should be affiliated to the Labour Party. He thought that this would not only secure the maximum solidarity within the Labour movement, but would also encourage the Communists to work through constitutional channels and abandon their notions of armed struggle. As an affiliated organisation, the CPGB would be forced to accept Labour Party standing orders and discipline, making it less likely to attack Labour policies and divide the workers. By alienating them the Labour leadership would not make their ideas or policies disappear; far better to incorporate them into a structure in which they could be controlled. As far as Maxton was concerned, then, the risks of continuing the isolation of the Communists were greater than accepting the Communists into membership. The Labour leadership were totally opposed to Maxton's reasoning. They argued that the CPGB's emphasis on the class war and violent revolution, together with membership of the Third International, put them at odds with the Labour Party constitution and the party's commitment to parliamentary institutions. This view was accepted by the majority of members and, in spite of repeated attempts, all affiliationist gestures towards Labour by the CPGB were rebuffed.

5

The rejection of revolution meant concentration on social reform and, while Maxton disliked the style of Allen's leadership of the ILP, it did not prevent him adopting his economic policies. The most important of these was the 'Living Wage' programme. The policy had been elaborated in a series of special reports to ILP conferences from 1924 onwards. The reports covered a wide terrain of economic subjects including land and agriculture, finance, unemployment, international trade and import boards. Most of this was non-controversial; it was only the 'Living Wage' proposals which generated any heat. The authors were H. N. Brailsford, J. A. Hobson, A. Creech Jones and E. F. Wise. It was, however, Hobson's underconsumptionist theories of depression and unemployment which provided the theoretical basis of the programme.

Hobson took a demand-deficient view of economic crisis and unemployment. He argued that the development of cartels and trusts had destroyed the free competition so beloved of nineteenth-century liberals and introduced highly restrictive economic competition. Control of markets allowed entrepreneurs to take a bigger than normal share of national income. This 'surplus' accruing to the Capitalists increasingly took the form of unearned income and upset the 'natural' balance between savings and investment. Too much was being saved and not enough was being invested. Wealth, therefore, was not being channelled into productive activities, but was being wasted in conspicuous consumption or hoarded or, worse still, being exported to more profitable investment opportunities abroad. This process led to a chronic tendency within the British economy to gluts and overproduction as the massive increase in the unearned income of the rich was incapable of consuming the constant increase in output. At the latter end of the social scale there was a crisis of under-consumption. The huge surplus accruing to the rich resulted in a low standard of living for the working class and their poverty and low wages, in turn, meant that there was a low level of demand for manufacturing products and services. The upshot of all this was that there was a positive disincentive to businessmen to invest their surplus wealth in British industry. To reverse these trends and regenerate the economy, Hobson advocated increasing the purchasing power of the masses through re-distributive taxation and higher minimum wages. To guard against the dangers of inflation following a general increase in incomes there was to be a policy of credit control exercised through the nationalisation of the Bank of England and those industries which were important in controlling the direction and pace of economic growth.

In spite of the change of title to Socialism In Our Time (SIOT), the analysis and the prescriptions were pre-Keynes rather than post-Marx. It was a gradualist programme aimed at erasing the worst defects of free market Capitalism. At the heart of the programme was the elimination of poverty rather than the destruction of the exploitative wage labour/capital relationship. Moreover, it was the increase of purchasing power as the way out of depression which took central place in the strategy. Nationalisation and other statutory controls were relegated to a subsidiary role. The main problem with the programme within the ILP was that it was open to misinterpretation. Some important sections of the party rejected it outright, for example, the Yorkshire Divisional Council, while others remained vague as to its significance for party policy. Oswald Mosley attacked it at the 1926 ILP Conference because its implementation would have involved the party in operating a Capitalist system of finance. Fenner Brockway at the same conference argued that the demand for a 'Living Wage' was unachievable inside a Capitalist society and all that it could do was to serve as a propaganda point to

win over the workers to the recognition that only the establishment of a Socialist society could provide them with a decent and
humane standard of living. Everyone seemed to be for it and
against it. Such was the confusion in the ILP that the 1928 Annual
Conference supported a resolution calling for the establishment
of a minimum wage which contradicted the high wage policy of
the SIOT programme. A minimum wage could be established on
the wage rate in the least efficient industry, whereas the 'Living
Wage' implied a maximum standard. Recognising the contradiction in the policy of the party, the NAC reformulated the 'Living
Wage' demand to apply immediately to government employees
and those working in firms receiving government money, with
the extension to all other industries in two years' time. The
trades unions opposed the programme, as they felt that wages
were not the concern of the ILP and that a state-operated wage
would pose a direct threat to the role of the unions in wage
bargaining. In spite of this kind of confusion and opposition from
various sections of the Labour movement and the ILP, Maxton
accepted the theory and programme uncritically and continued
to espouse it until his break with gradualism in 1928 with the
publication of the Cook/Maxton manifesto.

6

The adoption of the 'Living Wage' policy coincided with Maxton's
election as chairman of the ILP at the 1926 Conference. His
acceptance speech outlined in broad terms his idea of what the
party as a Socialist organisation should be doing and what his
role as leader ought to be. He said.:

> The ILP's duty is to hold the ultimate ideal [of socialism] clearly
> before the working class movement... Political success for the
> Labour Party is a certainty, but political success itself is a poor end
> unless, behind the Parliamentary majority, there is a determined
> revolutionary socialist opinion. It will be part of my duty to try to

make as far-reaching as possible this feeling which I believe is the feeling of the Party.'

Maxton, therefore, saw his task as leader of the ILP as that of promoting a greater movement towards fundamental social and economic change. However, Maxton did not view himself as a leader in the conventional sense. As John Paton, organising secretary of the ILP, once remarked, 'he declines to attempt to impose his will on the Party'. Maxton saw himself more as an agitator and rebel than as a leader or statesman. To him, the role of the leader was to express the will of the party as arrived at in debate and discussion. Although he did not always live up to the high standards set for him by others, his sense of fair play and his tolerant attitudes were sources of weakness in dealing with intra-party disputes but it was idealism which was his main deficiency as leader of the ILP. Parliamentary politics is necessarily about compromise and this he found difficult to come to terms with, especially when it involved sacrificing a principle. His unpragmatic approach made him an unwise choice as leader of a party committed to parliamentary politics and whose ideological base was essentially eclectic. What the ILP needed was someone who could unite the varying shades of political opinion within the organisation and maintain cordial links with the PLP and the unions. Although he claimed in *Forward* shortly before his election as Chairman, that he would use his influence to 'prevent the movement being split up over disputes between Rights and Lefts', Maxton was the wrong man to perform this task. As events were later to prove, Maxton drove deeper wedges between the various wings of the ILP

There were also deeper political and structural problems which the ILP had to face, regardless of who the leader might be. Within the Labour Party the power of the trades unions was increasingly important in determining conference policy and the political careers of aspiring Labour leaders. The ILP, through its separate spheres policy, was totally devoid of a base within the trades union movement and was, therefore, incapable of drawing support from this crucial part of the Labour movement – something which was clearly demonstrated in its failure to win support for the 'Living Wage' proposals. Moreover, there was the problem that, as Labour was seen as a party of government, it was natural that the politically aspiring should gravitate towards that part of the movement where power and patronage was held and this, with Maxton's election, ceased to be in the ILP. Membership declined from the moment the Labour Party was seen as more than just a loose federation of different interests and began to be organised on an efficient district and constituency level. When Maxton was elected Chairman the number of branches stood at 1075. Just three years later the number had fallen to 746 and decline was occurring in every divisional council. Even before 1926 the Liberal element which had been grouped around the Union of Democratic Control during the First World War had gone over to Labour in 1924. After this, middle-class support steadily ebbed away to the Labour Party denying the ILP their skill and knowledge. What increased the squeeze on the ILP was the fact that the Communists were a serious rival for the dissident left-wing elements in the Labour movement. The ILP could no longer claim to be the natural home of the left. The problems facing Maxton then were quite substantial, although at the time perhaps not fully appreciated.

His election as Chairman was, however, warmly approved by the ILP's left wing. Michael Marcus, writing in the *ILP Journal* (May 1926), expressed the feelings of the rank and file when he claimed that 'with James Maxton as propagandist and moulder of policy the Party will yet achieve great and lasting things which will surpass all previous efforts. . . and lead us to Socialism in our time'. Perhaps more predicatably, John Wheatley declared that 'there is no man more likely to lead the British people into a socialist state of society than Maxton'. The view from the right of the party was, as one might expect, not so enthusiastic. In a letter to Fred Jowett some years later, Phillip Snowden confessed that 'When Maxton was made chairman of the ILP I had a conviction that he would ruin the party, and he has succeeded in this better than I expected'.[10]

What Snowden failed to realise was that Maxton's election was symptomatic of the rank and file of the ILP's dissatisfaction with the gradualist policies that he and others like Allen and Mac-Donald believed in. Maxton as Chairman of the ILP heralded a new mood of militancy in the party and this coincided with a leftward turn in the Labour movement. It was Maxton, and not Snowden, who was running at this moment with the changing tide of optimism in Labour circles and it was not long before the General Strike of May 1926 would put this to the test.

5 The General Strike and its aftermath

The General Strike of 1926 was the culmination of a process of deteriorating relations between the miners, the coal-owners and government which stretched back into the immediate post-war period. During the war the mines had been taken into public control and the miners wished this arrangement to become permanent, especially after the Sankey Commission of 1919 had come out in favour of nationalisation. However, the Commission's recommendations were rejected by the Lloyd George government and this led to a strike in September 1920. As part of a pre-war agreement with the railway and transport unions, the strike was to signal action by other members of what was known as the Triple Alliance (TA) but the other members of the TA failed to support the miners and only delayed the strike taking place. The national coal strike began on 16 October and lasted three weeks. The outcome represented a partial victory for the miners with wage increases being won, although the amount was to be dependent on greater productivity. The small improvement in wages was soon almost completely wiped out. A fall in coal exports encouraged the government to speed up the timetable for the transfer of the mines back to private ownership. On taking over on 31 March 1920, the coal-owners immediately made cuts in wages. The miners refused to accept the reductions and were locked out by the employers. There was a strike threat by the TA but this was withdrawn on 15 April – an event known as 'Black Friday'. The miners suffered a crushing defeat and returned to work at the end of June on the employers' terms. This defeat of the miners signalled a general offensive against wages in other industries. The trades unions were powerless to resist in the face of falling membership and economic depression.

The election of the first Labour government saw the introduction of a Miners' Minimum Wages Bill but this was forestalled by the owners voluntarily granting a substantial wage increase. Before this agreement expired in the summer of 1925, the MacDonald government had been defeated and coal prices and sales had slumped. The employers once more resorted to cost cutting by reducing wages to their 1921-4 level and increasing the length of the working day from seven to eight hours. The General Council of the TUC threw its weight behind the miners and the transport and railway workers agreed to impose an embargo on the movement of coal. Faced with this threat, the government climbed down and offered a temporary subsidy to maintain existing wages and standard profits. Meanwhile, another royal commission – the Samuel Commission – was set up to seek ways of improving the efficiency of the industry. Its recommendations included the nationalisation of mining royalties, reorganisation of the industry, better working consultation and more research. However, it had little to say on the immediate problems facing the coal industry other than to recommend cuts in wages, no increase in working hours and a national wage scale. The report pleased no one and it was ignored by all parties in the dispute.

It was obvious to most observers that the subsidy was designed to provide the government with a breathing space in which to build up coal stocks and make contingency plans for the movement of food supplies and essential raw materials. The country was divided into ten areas and each placed under the control of a civil commissioner. An Emergency Committee of Supply and Transport was set up and a private strike-breaking organisation, the Organisation for the Maintenance of Supplies, was launched to supply blackleg labour. The Baldwin government also took the precaution of arresting eleven leading members of the GPGB on a charge of sedition on 17 October 1925. This ensured that there was no alternative leadership to that of the official Labour leadership. The General Council in contrast had made no plans and the Labour movement was, therefore, ill-prepared when the miners were locked out at the end of April 1926 following the expiry of the mining subsidy. The TUC, with the memory of 'Black Friday' clearly in front of it, decided to call its members in support of the miners on 3 May.

The response of the workers to the TUC's call to strike was by any standards enthusiastic. But the strike was only to last nine days. At the time of greatest support the General Council inexplicably ordered a return to work. The pretext for calling off the action was that, in the opinion of the General Council, a memorandum drawn up by Sir Herbert Samuel constituted the basis for a settlement. The memorandum called for the introduction of a National Wages Board which would undertake to reduce wages but only when the recommendations for the reorganisation of the coal industry made by the 1925 Commission were effectively adopted. On this basis the TUC called off the strike without consulting the miners and with no assurances from the government or coal-owners.

2

The collapse of what was class conflict on a grand scale led to the cry among those on the left that the General Council had betrayed the working class. This was Maxton's view. Although ill for much of 1926 – the result of a duodenal ulcer – Maxton addressed several meetings during the strike. On 2 May he urged the workers at a demonstration in Glasgow to support the miners but he also warned them against doing anything which might provoke a violent response from the state. When the strike was over he pilloried the government and the TUC. According to Maxton's analysis, the strike had represented a political challenge to the constitution and in the context he thought this right. The Baldwin government's handling of the strike had been an example of naked class rule but the TUC had been unwilling to mobilise worker power against it. The General Council had sold out at the crucial moment to the status quo. Its attempts at negotiation were interpreted as signs of weakness and not strength by those in power. Thus militant and class-conscious workers were, in Maxton's view, let down by a timid and reformist leadership.

Maxton's analysis represents not only a misreading of the role of the General Council in the strike but also a failure to ask important questions regarding the political implications of the dispute for his own philosophy of Socialism. Compromise and negotiation had been the aim of the TUC before the strike began and this continued to be its policy while the dispute was in progress. When the TUC embarked on a course of confrontation with the government it was felt that the strike would last only a matter of days. However, the government proved far more stubborn than the TUC had expected and when the former began to talk in terms of threats to the constitution, the General Council eagerly accepted the opportunity presented by the Samuel memorandum to call off the strike. To have continued it indefinitely against a determined government would have eventually provoked a constitutional crisis of massive proportions. This was something a reformist leadership could not hope to deal with. The only alternative was the CPGB but it was too small, too ineffective and, in any case, its leading members were in gaol. The rest of the Labour movement, including Maxton and the ILP, was too convinced of the parliamentary road to Socialism to mount a syndicalist challenge for political power. Moreover, as a study of the left-wing press in Britain would show, no party of the left had developed a theory in which a general strike could be used as an instrument to bring about Socialism. The best that could be hoped for in the circumstances was another general election and the return of a Labour government. Significantly, the latter was the only serious demand made by the CPGB during those nine days in May.

The general return to work saw the miners isolated and forced to fight on alone. After eight months their resolve was broken by hunger and they returned to work on the employers' conditions. The whole episode proved a disaster for the trades union movement as membership fell to under five million for the first time since 1916. Before 1926 industrial disputes had involved an average of more than one million workers a year; in the ten years afterwards they never involved more than 300,000. The mood for the movement changed from confrontation to conciliation. Apart from the government and the coal-owners, the real winner was the Labour Party. The failure of the General Strike marked the end of the influence of syndicalism in the Labour movement and the triumph of parliamentarianism. It was to be parliament and not the industrial struggle which was to be the future motive force in bringing about economic and social justice. Ramsay MacDonald summed up the new political direction of the Labour movement when he declared that 'the weapon of the General Strike is no good – even less now than ever'.

The mood of defeatism, or realism as some would have it, was not one that Maxton could easily accept. The lesson he had drawn from the strike was not the same as that of the official leadership. Maxton saw the experience as indicative of the 'latent power' of the organised working class. The strike's failure did not signify the end of mass working-class action, rather it marked its beginning. Speaking in public for the first time since his illness,

69

although legally banned from doing so under the Emergency Powers Act, Maxton urged striking miners – somewhat unrealistically – to 'prepare for an even bigger fight than this'. Shortly after this he visited Derbyshire with Kirkwood to address the miners. While there, both men came into conflict with the police as Maxton tried to defy the ban on him from speaking at Staveley. During the incident Kirkwood was arrested and appeared in court on 15 November accompanied by Maxton, Tom Johnston, Campbell Stephen and Neil Maclean. Maxton was ordered to be silent by the court and eventually told to leave. His repeated outbursts caused the case to be adjourned; a decison which was greeted with wild enthusiasm by a crowd who had gathered outside the courthouse singing *The Red Flag*. The cheering crowds followed the Clydesiders to the station where Kirkwood addressed them before catching the train. Kirkwood was later fined twenty-five pounds. This incident was symptomatic of Maxton's belief that 'If the spokesmen of Labour... can maintain and develop the same spirit of courage and self-sacrifice... a few years should give the workers... peace and power'.

The government thought otherwise. In June 1927 the Trades Disputes Act was passed, which made illegal the 'general' or 'sympathetic' strike and also changed the system whereby trade unionists paid their political levy to the Labour Party from one of contracting out to one of contracting in, hoping that this would lead to a fall in affiliated members. During the debate on the third reading of the Bill, Maxton was suspended from the Commons for calling the Attorney-General, Sir Douglas Hogg, a 'blackguard and a liar'. Churchill moved his suspension which was carried by a large majority. However, trades unionists were not the only ones to suffer from this reactionary Tory backlash. In November of that year the Unemployed Insurance Bill threatened to cut relief to certain classes of claimants considered to be 'not genuinely seeking work'. Maxton was once more suspended from the Commons for using the word 'damned' during the debate on the legislation. Anglo/Soviet relations also suffered when in May 200 policemen raided the offices of the Soviet trade organisation, Arcos, in London looking for incriminating evidence against Communists. Nothing was found but the government, to save face, decided to break off diplomatic relations with the Soviet Union.

Maxton felt that the heavy-handed repressive tactics of government, intended to cripple the Labour movement, would rebound on it and create conditions for revolution. Writing in the *New Leader* in September 1927, he outlined the political analysis which had led to this optimistic conclusion:

> The government by force had crushed the miners down to starvation level, had proceeded to cripple the constitutional weapons of the trade unions and the PLP, which the workers had created as their means to economic betterment and freedom, and were now proceeding to alter the balance of the Constitution... so entrenching the wealthy in their power. If they succeeded in their efforts in rivetting poverty permanently on the mass of the people, and placing themselves permanently in a dominant position of wealth and power, they were setting up conditions that made revolution inevitable.

Therefore, the more repressive the actions of the government, the more Maxton felt that it would become apparent to the working class that Capitalism was not in its interest. However, while Maxton was determined to maintain the same mood of militancy which had led to the General Strike, the trades union leaders were preaching industrial peace.

3

Faced with falling membership and income, the trades unions adopted a more collaborationist policy towards capital. The new mood was symbolised in the Mond/Turner talks of 1927/8. The talks were initiated by a letter sent from Sir Alfred Mond (Lord

Melchett) to the President of the TUC, George Hicks, after the latter had made a conciliatory speech at the 59th Congress in Edinburgh. The letter invited the General Council to a conference to discuss the whole issue of industrial organisation and industrial relations. The meeting took place on 12 January 1928 and a wide range of questions were debated, including the finance and management of industry, new developments in technology, the setting up of a National Industrial Council and conciliatory machinery for settling disputes, as well as methods of rationalising industry. This was the first of twelve such conferences which took place in the period up to July. The Mond/Turner talks, as they were known, were approved overwhelmingly by the TUC at its 60th Congress.

It was this new policy of class collaboration which Maxton set out to attack and ultimately destroy. The chosen method was to be the publication of a manifesto addressed to the 'Workers of Britain' and a nation-wide campaign of demonstrations and meetings. The Cook/Maxton manifesto called for the working class to engage in an unceasing war against Capitalism and the Mond/Turner talks. In some accounts the origin of the manifesto is said to have been the work of Wheatley; in others, Gallacher is given the responsibility for drafting it. However, it does seem as if it was the CPGB which took the lead in introducing A. J. Cook, the miners' leader, to Maxton. As we have seen, Maxton had for some time been sympathetic to Communist affiliation to the Labour Party and in 1927 at the ILP's Leicester Conference went so far as to argue for the unification of the Third International and the Labour and Socialist International (LSI) to 'secure the international solidarity of labour'. Thus he was amenable to approaches from the Communists. At a meeting in the Commons, which included Wheatley, Gallacher, Buchanan, Kirkwood and Scanlon, the Cook/Maxton manifesto was drawn up and issued towards the end of June 1928.

The manifesto was supplemented by the publication of a pamphlet by Cook and Maxton, *Our Case for a Socialist Revival*, which spelt out in greater detail their alternative political strategy. The authors saw the Labour movement as fragmented and, because of this, unable to resist the increasing centralisation and power of capital. The rationalisation proposal of the Mond/Turner talks would lead to a greater ratio of fixed capital to labour and result in a shake out of the workforce, which in turn would mean further fragmentation and weakness. The response of Labour to these proposals had to be one of united opposition; there was to be no room for sectional or separatist tendencies. The centralisation of capital had to be matched by the centralisation of working-class power. This involved, Cook and Maxton argued, restructuring and overhauling the machinery of working-class organisation. The trades unions had to organise themselves along industrial rather than craft or occupational lines; bigger and not smaller units of organisation were needed. From this point the unions were urged to build close links with the unemployed to prevent blacklegging in strikes and counter the intimidation of the employed workforce by the employers, while co-operative societies would support the unions in disputes by seeing to it that, unlike the miners, they were not starved back to work. Cook and Maxton also advocated greater political tolerance, which would allow all parts of the Labour movement to join in the united struggle against Capitalism. Specifically, this meant allowing Communists to hold union offices and to act as delegates to Labour Party conferences. A united Labour movement fighting on a Socialist programme, the authors claimed, would be strong enough to defeat the organised power of capital. As part of their immediate programme they called for the nationalisation without compensation of the banks, land, mines and railways, the abolition of all incomes over £5,000 and the dissolution of the monarchy.

With its emphasis on the class struggle and the destruction

of Capitalism, the manifesto was more radical than SIOT and, as such, received enormous publicity in the Capitalist press. Maxton declared with characteristic optimism that, 'there's going to be no failure, but success. This campaign is going to bring together a body of men and women that'll save the soul of the working class movement'.[11] To launch the manifesto a meeting was organised at St Andrew's Hall, Glasgow. However, a lack-lustre performance by Maxton was a sign of things to come. Although the nation-wide campaign of meetings was successful, with standing room only in many cases, the movement itself was a failure. Gallacher claims it was Maxton's refusal to use a speech he had written for him, and use instead a 'cliché-ridden' one of his own, which was the principle reason for failure but it was really more to do with the widespread opposition within the Labour movement.

The manifesto had been published without the approval of the NAC of the ILP. Maxton, rather disingeniously, claimed that he was acting on his own initiative in appending his signature to the document, although as Chairman of the party he could not have been unaware that his action appeared to commit the ILP to the policy and programme of the campaign. For this reason he was called to appear before the NAC at a special meeting in London on 30 June to explain his conduct. There was strong criticism from delegates from Yorkshire, Wales, Scotland and London, with only Lancasire among the divisional councils enthusiastic. The main thrust of the attack on Maxton was led by Dollan and Shinwell. What concerned them most was not the spirit of the manifesto but the decision of Maxton to act outside the party and 'the calling of unofficial conferences' with non-party members.[12] Maxton was urged to work within the ILP and through the Labour Party to achieve SIOT. Dollan moved a resolution to this effect, seconded by John Scurr, but it was defeated by six votes to eight. At the Scottish Council of the

ILP's special meeting seven days later, at which Maxton was present, the resolution was carried. Maxton stated, somewhat contradictorily, that he did not think the manifesto 'a big enough thing to put before the NAC' and that he was simply 'stating party policy and as time was short he did not feel it necessary to get preliminary endorsement'.

After making stinging attacks on the current Labour leadership, Maxton and Wheatley were also censured by the PLP at its meeting on 19 July. Further criticism came at the 1928 Labour Party Conference when MacDonald attacked those responsible for the issue of 'independent and unauthorised manifestoes'. Even the CPGB, which had played a leading part in initiating the campaign, was critical. The manifesto was described as 'weak and sentimental', in spite of Gallacher's alleged authorship. By the time it was issued,the CPGB, following changes in Comintern policy, began to attack Social Democrats as 'social fascists'. The new 'class against class' line involved trying to encourage trades unions to disaffiliate from the Labour Party and urging workers not to vote for Labour in elections. The Cook/Maxton manifesto was thus seen from the new Communist strategy as an attempt by a 'pseudo-left opposition to divert workers away from the Communist Party' and therefore had to be 'mercilessly' exposed.[13]

The attack from the official Labour movement with its references to 'unofficial conferences', as well as several statements made at the time by Maxton, Wheatley and others, has given rise to speculation over whether the campaign was a preliminary to the launching of a new party. This was the view expressed in some of the contemporary Liberal/Conservative journals. The *Saturday Review* shrewdly asked the question of whether Maxton would form a separate organisation, following his failure to win over the Labour movement. Indeed, this was at the back of Wheatley's mind from the outset of the campaign. Both Brockway and Paton have stated that Wheatley was in favour of forming a new party and that the Cook/Maxton manifesto meetings were a means of sounding out opinion on this issue. The issuing of pledge cards at meetings seems to further support this proposition as they were intended to 'produce a register of people' who believed in the project and who could be relied upon if necessary to provide a nucleus of support for such a venture. These cadres would be pledged only to work for Labour candidates with Socialist credentials which in time, if no new organisation emerged, would remove the existing leadership. Added to these organisational goals were the scathing attacks Wheatley made on MacDonald and Thomas during the campaign, all of which points to the conclusion that if Wheatley did not desire the setting up of a new party, then he certainly desired a massive restructuring of the leadership of the Labour Party.

Whether Maxton went the whole way with Wheatley is open to question. As Scanlon noted in his polemical study of the Labour Party, Maxton opposed Wheatley, arguing that the Labour movement would resist anything which threatened to damage the prospects of Labour at the next General Election. At the inaugural meeting of the campaign in Glasgow, Maxton avoided making any remarks which could have been interpreted as an attack on the Labour Party. When pressed by local Communist, Aitken Ferguson, on the question of whether he would lead a movement to expel Ramsay MacDonald from the Labour Party, Maxton's reply was evasive. He said that 'he stood for toleration of both left and right wings in the movement' and added that he would do nothing which 'would lead to his own expulsion from the Labour Party'. Maxton was also of the opinion that the manifesto campaign would put Labour back into office. Answering critics at the ILP summer school in August 1928, he declared that the 'protest was made at the opportune moment, so that it would not wreck Labour's prospects at the next General Election'. It was his failure to condemn outright MacDonald and the Labour

Party which led to repeated attacks on him by the CPGB. Perhaps it was also why Wheatley, who agreed to underwrite the cost of the campaign, tore up his cheque after the first meeting.

What in essence Maxton was trying to achieve was to get the Labour movement to break with gradualism. The Fabian philosophy of step-by-step change was too slow for Maxton. The danger was that it led Labour to administer Capitalism while at the same time trying to dismantle it. The two tasks were incompatible and would result, argued Maxton, in the Labour Party degenerating into a 'petty social reform movement'. Maxton believed that Labour could not run the Capitalist system any more successfully than the Tories. The task of Socialists was to transform society, not to patch it up through piecemeal social reforms. Thus the campaign for Maxton was not so much aimed at setting up a new Labour party, but at re-awakening the existing one to its fundamental principles and philosophy. However, all he had done was to increase opposition and suspicion in the Labour movement regarding his motives and policies; feelings which would intensify during the lifetime of the second Labour government.

6   *The second Labour government*

1

The movement towards a more militantly left-wing position in the ILP led to the resignation of leading ILPers, with MacDonald and Snowden among the more prominent. Consequently, the ILP was a party split between those loyal to MacDonald and the Labour Party and those who supported SIOT and were critical of, or in outright opposition to, the Labour leadership. Among the former was Dr Alfred Salter, MP for Bermondsey, who, along with William Leach MP, the leader of the Bradford ILP, organised a meeting in November 1928 of twenty-eight ILP MPs to proclaim support for MacDonald and declare that the 'ILP had outlived its usefulness'. What, asked the critics, was the need for a party within a party, particularly when the ILP was so critical of Labour policy?

Maxton was faced with the task of reaffirming the need for the ILP as a distinctive force within the Labour movement. In an important article in the *Socialist Review* (March 1928), he argued that the ILP was not simply an educational and propaganda organisation within the Labour movement but a body whose duty it was to:

> preach the principles and ideals of Socialism, to devise methods, plans and schemes for the achievement of Socialism, to encourage, and even on occasion to goad the other working class organisations to bigger aims and stronger demands. . . It must hold out to them (workers) the hope of speedy release from servitude, but it must

also show them that speed is conditioned by. . . the power of the workers to organise solidly, to visualise clearly, and stick tenaciously to their object.

This role necessarily involved policy-making and a leading part in seeing those policies implemented by a future Labour government.

But the question posed by the Salter group was not without substance. Maxton had shown a strong desire to lead the ILP away from reformism and had actively sought an alternative mechanism for doing so. Since his election as Chairman, the NAC had exercised a greater control over the actions of the ILP parliamentary group. This new direction began at a special meeting of the parliamentary group in March 1926 when Fenner Brockway proposed that the full group of MPs should meet only occasionally, while a small committee of NAC MPs, that is, Kirkwood, Maxton, Stephen, Scurr, Stanford, Wallhead and two others, would meet regularly to lay down overall ILP strategy in the Commons. This was accepted without much comment as, in any case, these meetings were not well attended. From this point onwards, these seven members directed the ILP MPs in parliament. In 1928 Maxton further attempted to extend his control over the party MPs when he set up a group of twenty-eight MPs to whom the ILP would be financially responsible and who, in return, would be expected to support ILP policy in the Commons – the essence of which was SIOT. A coherent and recognisable ILP voice in the Labour Party and in the Commons was the core of Maxton's strategy.

One of the objects of the Maxton group was to oppose the 1928 Labour Party programme – *Labour and the Nation*. The new programme was the antithesis of the radicalism of the ILP's 'Living Wage' proposals. Speaking at the 1928 Brimingham Conference of the Labour Party, Maxton said of the programme that:

the whole formation of it, the utterances of those who have been
most strongly defending it, lead one to the conclusion that they are
looking at their responsibilities as if the approach to Socialism was
to be a long, slow process of gradualistic, peaceful parliamentary
change. I have sat and watched a Tory Government for four-and-a-
half years trying to run Capitalism. . . and they have been unable
to make any impression on any one of the big outstanding problems. . . In every essential direction the condition of this country
has got worse. . . A Labour Government cannot run Capitalism any
more successfully than Baldwin and the others.

As far as Maxton was concerned, even if a Labour government
could carry out all the proposals contained in *Labour and the
Nation* it would still only amount to 'controlled capitalism', it
would not bring Socialism any nearer. Any Labour government
coming into office with a majority, Maxton argued, should at
the very least consider the nationalisation of the banks, land,
mines and railways, as well as import and export controls, as its
first priority. The programme outlined in *Labour and the Nation*
was not only unsocialist but, when compared with the keynesian-
like manifesto of the Liberal Party, *We Can Conquer Unemployment*,
it was conservative and unimaginative.

At the heart of the Liberal manifesto was the industrial regen-
eration of Britain. This was also an important part of Maxton's
economic strategy. The key to greater domestic investment and,
hence, employment lay, he argued, in securing control of finance
capital. From his study of Capitalism and no doubt from his
reading of Hobson's classic text, *Imperialism: A Study* (1902), Maxton had concluded that the interests of finance capital were not
identical to those of industrial capital. The Tory government's
policy had been geared towards promoting the interests of the
City against manufacturing industry, of which the return to gold
in 1925 was but one example. Maxton, like Hobson earlier, was

of the view that the British economy had reached a stage where finance capital had become parasitic on the hard-working and 'honest' producing classes. As the banking system had failed to meet the needs of industry, Maxton advocated the nationalisation of the Bank of England in order that the savings of the country could be used to assist industrial recovery. State control of banking would also be extended to cover foreign trade. Maxton opposed the protectionism of the Tories and the free trade of the Liberal and Labour Parties and called for the bulk buying of imports and the bulk selling of exports with other countries. The arrangements were to be made through periodic international conferences of heads of state. The socialisation of banking and industry was then to be supplemented by the socialisation of world trade.

Maxton's economic analysis and prescriptions for recovery were not too dissimilar to those propounded by Oswald Mosley. His economic views were developed in conversations with Keynes and outlined in a pamphlet, *Revolution by Reason*, in 1925. Like Maxton, Mosley rejected the notion that evolutionary Socialism, as articulated by the Fabians, was relevant in a situation of economic crisis. Instead he advocated an emergency policy of credit expansion through the nationalisation of the Bank of England. The increase in credit would be channelled towards the workers who would use their higher purchasing power to boost demand in the domestic economy and, as workers were likely to buy necessities rather than luxuries, credit expansion would have the added bonus of providing a stimulus to the recovery of the depressed staple industries. To guard against the inflationary effects of this financial strategy, Mosley advocated state planning of the economy. During the lifetime of the second Laour government, Mosley, along with Jimmy Thomas and Tom Johnston, was part of the government's employment team. His dissatisfaction with Labour's poor efforts to solve the economic crisis led to the circulation of the 'Mosley Memorandum' which, amongst other things, advocated the general lines of strategy laid down in the 1925 pamphlet, within the Cabinet and, later, within the PLP. Mosley's radical economic strategy was rejected by both groups, although a resolution to reconsider its proposals was only narrowly defeated at the 1930 Labour Party Conference. In December of that year Mosley issued a 'Manifesto' which was signed by only seventeen Labour MPs, some of whom were close associates of Maxton and A. J. Cook. The derisory response from the Labour movement convinced Mosley to leave the Labour Party and to form the New Party in February 1931, which later became the Fascist party. However, in the event, he was actually expelled by Labour.

Thus Maxton was not alone in challenging Labour's reliance on increasingly outmoded economic thinking. However, whether Maxton's, or Mosley's, economic strategy was practicable in an economy in crisis in debateable. Taking run-down staple industries like textiles, coal, steel and shipbuilding into public ownership would not have increased employment, particularly when the market for their products was so depressed. State control of banking would have been effective in harnessing savings but, if Britain's economic problems lay in the area of structural decline, manipulation of monetary indicators and exchange rates would not have made much difference to the problem. Moreover, in terms of Socialist objectives Maxton was still prepared to leave a large part of industry in private hands. However, the boldness of the ILP programme contrasted sharply with the liking of Snowden for sound finance and balanced budgets. It was also an indication that the Labour Party was beginning to disintegrate into warring factions as unemployment kept on increasing and the official Labour leadership had no positive response.

2

The General Election of 1929 saw Labour returned as the largest party but without an overall majority. The election campaign demonstrated how much Labour was a party which grounded its appeal in pragmatic reform rather than full-blooded Socialism. It was estimated that only six per cent of Labour's election addresses mentioned 'Socialism', while forty-three per cent of Conservative addresses did. Given this, it was not surprising that few on Labour's left wing found a place in the new Cabinet. In an earlier draft list for 1929, Wheatley had been pencilled in as first choice for the Ministry of Labour and Maxton as second choice for Paymaster General. With Maxton and Wheatley in open revolt their inclusion was unlikely. Moreover, given the experience of the first minority Labour Government, Maxton felt it tactically wrong to repeat the exercise. By adopting a radical social programme, such as that contained in SIOT, Labour would have been able to put the issue squarely to the country – Socialism or Capitalism? A Tory/Liberal government would have been forced into the task of running a system in crisis which would lead, as unemployment reached record levels, to the growth of an active, militant movement behind Labour. Taking office on minority terms was tantamount to accepting responsibility for the economic crisis.

Maxton had also come out against cabinet-style government as an inadequate instrument for transforming Capitalism and administering Socialism. However, when asked by the *New Leader* for his reaction to the personnel for the new government, Maxton replied that, although he did not agree with its programme in full, he would watch 'the government apply it in the most friendly spirit'. This was to be a constant dilemma for the Maxton group; they were opposed to the government's policies but were afraid to take the responsibility for the fall of the government. Even when their impatience with the government's inability to react in a positive way to growing unemployment and economic depression was at its greatest, they refused, in spite of repeated opportunities, to vote with the opposition on motions of censure.

The first sign of opposition to the Labour government came in an amendment to the King's speech in the summer of 1929 in the names of Wise, Wheatley, Stephen, Lee, Kirkwood and Maxton. The amendment demanded that every man should have an 'income, including children's allowances, sufficient to meet the human needs of himself and his family' and called on the government to introduce measures 'aiming at the re-organisation of the industrial system, so that it shall provide for the needs of the community, by nationalising the key sources of industrial power'. This bold policy was designed to prevent MacDonald from reaching an understanding with the Liberals and, as such, it was a failure. By December 1929 Maxton was proclaiming that he was not responsible for the government's policies as neither he nor the ILP nor the PLP had been consulted on membership of the Cabinet.

Maxton emerged as the foremost critic of the government. He criticised the Coal Mines Bill of 1930 for failing to provide a minimum wage for miners and attacked it over other issues including the Education Bill, National Health Insurance, Representation of the People, Public Loans, and so on. Most of all, however, he criticised Labour for not doing enough for the unemployed. Maxton and his group of ILP MPs had made the crucial test of their continued support for the MacDonald government, not the introduction of Socialism, as in the circumstances this was recognised as unlikely, but its treatment of those out of work, whose numbers were growing all the time as manufacturing output fell to record levels. His first objective in this field was the abolition of the 'not genuinely seeking work' (NGSW) clause in the Unemployed Insurance Act. His second was the raising of the scales of benefit paid to the unemployed. The NGSW clause was an offensive piece of legislation, particulary in times of high unemployment, and was strongly opposed by the trades unions. The Maxton group in the Commons argued that if a man registered for work at the Employment Exchange, that in itself would be proof of his desire to become gainfully employed. They fought against the subjective element in the Unemployment Insurance Bill which allowed disqualification of the right to benefit on the basis of the officer's assessment of the 'applicant's state of mind'. Other objections were aimed at the Bill's failure to alter the scales of benefit to any significant degree. These were set at 32s a week for a man, wife and three children. This contradicted the election of pledge of Labour to provide work or maintenance and was contrary to the scale of 45s a week which the Labour movement had supported in its evidence to the Blanesborough Committee of 1924. Although the trades union officials had no time for the antics of the Maxton group, their opposition to the NGSW clause was used by Maxton to pressurise the MacDonald government into amending the offending legislation in such a way that the onus of proof was on the Employment Exchange and not on the claimant. However, they were less successful when it came to raising the level of unemployment benefit.

These clashes with the government over unemployment legislation were mild in comparison with the furore created in the Labour movement over Maxton's opposition to the 'Anomalies' (Unemployment Insurance No. 3) Bill in July 1931. The Bill was designed to end what were considered as growing abuses of the benefit system, however, the legislation hit hardest at those in casual work and, in particular, married women. These classes of claimants were denied the right to benefit. What was even more annoying to the left was the fact that the Bill carried into effect most of the recommendations of the Holman Gregory Commission, whose establishment in December 1930 was the cause of intense bitterness between Margaret Bondfield, Minister of Labour, and the TUC. The Bill was defended by Labour MPs on the basis that it was only intended to remove 'spongers' from the unemployed register. The official position was summed up by Labour loyalist J. E. Mills, MP for Dartford, when he claimed that the Bill was to stop 'wangling', which was deeply resented by a 'majority of our people', even more bitterly than by 'our political opponents'. Maxton and the ILP saw it as a question of work or maintenance, something promised in successive Labour Party manifestoes. With other Clydeside MPs Maxton forced an all-night sitting in the Commons on 15/6 July in an attempt to have the Bill talked-out but in the end they had to admit defeat. Maxton said of his stand that night: 'There has been a grand coalition here but if I never do another thing in public life, I am glad that I stood here through the night exposing that great united attack on the poor people.'

3

Although generally supportive of MacDonald's foreign policy in recognising the Soviet Union and bringing about a (temporary) reduction in the world's arsenal, Maxton was highly critical of the government's policy towards the British Empire. In his mind the existence of the Empire not only constituted a denial of self-government to the oppressed colonial peoples but also provided a rationale for peacetime standing armies and large amounts of expenditure on armaments. Organisational expression of his opposition to Imperialism was reflected in his membership of the Communist-inspired and dominated League Against Imperialism (LAI). The League was an international body. The British section was formed on 8 April 1927 after a meeting in the Commons and Fenner Brockway was elected its first Chairman. However, as the LAI was opposed by the Social Democrat LSI, to retain his seat on the Executive of the latter Brockway had to resign from the LAI. Maxton replaced him as chairman in October of that year in an individual capacity.

The League fought Imperialism all over the world but the main focus of its attention at this time was independence for India. In a deliberately provocative act the LAI held a meeting in November 1928 supporting self-determination for the Indian peoples and attacking Labour's decision to participate in the Simon Commission, which was set up to consider and, ultimately, reject self-government for India. The meeting was held in the constituency of Labour's representative on the Commission, Clement Attlee, with Maxton in the chair. A resolution was passed condemning Attlee's membership. However, it was disowned by Maxton. In a letter to the Executive of the Labour Party he disassociated himself from the Limehouse resolution and gave an assurance that he would exercise care to 'avoid finding himself in a similar position in the future'. He still favoured independence for India but realised that that could only come with the election of a Labour government. This explanation was accepted by the Executive and the matter was dropped. Five months later Maxton signed a leaflet issued by the LAI attacking the Tory government's action against the Bombay textile workers' union during the strike there and calling for an embargo by British workers against the movement of munitions and troops to India.

As chairman of the British section, he was one of the representatives at the Second Congress of the League in July 1929 in Frankfurt. Maxton was made President at the Congress and was strongly criticised by the LSI for accepting the position. The Executive of the LSI saw the participation of Maxton as 'of the highest strategical value [to the Communists]'. Under the presidency of Maxton 'the *purely Bolshevik* character of the *real* leadership of the League' would be concealed from the workers.[14] These charges were repeated in *Forward* without revealing the source. After some trouble gaining access to Belgium, Maxton made an incredibly high-handed speech to the LAI delegates in Frankfurt, which seemed to confirm the worst fears of the LSI. He declared: 'There are elements in the ILP who do not support my anti-imperialist policy and tactics, and my association with the League. They may even be a majority of the Party, but I am Chairman of the Party and will fight for the adoption of a militant policy against imperialism, and those in the ranks of the Party who wish a moderate reformist policy will be discarded'.[15]

Maxton was ordered by the two international secretaries of the LAI, Munzenberg and Chattopadhajaya, and the British section of the League to reprint the speech in the *New Leader*. Maxton replied in one word – 'No'. Another letter followed demanding that he publish the Frankfurt speech and express public disagreement with the policy of the Labour government towards Egypt, India and Palestine. Maxton continued to defy the League, saying that he did not 'intend to be bullied, harassed and pestered as to his times and methods by which he should express himself'. At a meeting of the Executive of the British section of the LAI on 17 September 1929 Maxton was expelled for actions incompatible with its principles. Writing in the *Sunday Worker* (1 September 1929), Gallacher previously and incredibly claimed that Maxton's membership of the LAI was for the sole purpose of 'sabotaging its activities' and accused him further of helping the Labour government to re-establish 'the prestige of the British Empire'. Maxton's expulsion was followed by the resignations of A. J. Cook, T. I. Mardy Jones MP and Dorothy Jewson. From Gallacher's utterances, the expulsion of Maxton was less to do with his conduct and more to do with the adoption of the 'class against class' strategy of the CPGB. Indeed, in a letter to the 11th Congress of the CPGB, Comintern described Maxton as one of the 'sham left representatives of social fascism'.[16] From November 1929 onwards the LAI was designated a proscribed organisation by the Labour Party.

Expulsion from the LAI in no way dampened Maxton's enthusiasm for self-government for India. At the 1930 Labour Party Conference the idea of dominion status for India was attacked by the ILP. An amendment was moved calling for self-determination and an end to the repression of nationalist forces but Maxton was careful to exphasise that the satisfaction of nationalist aspirations was not an end in itself; there were also class aspirations to be met. Following the report of the Round Table talks, Maxton made his views on the subject of Indian self-government more explicit, stating:

> I am not primarily concerned with Indian nationalist independence. India, I think should rule itself. . . My concern is. . . in the struggle of the poor people, the working classes, for economic and social liberation. . . that section in India who do not believe that Indian self-government will abolish poverty among the Indian people, who are prepared to agree that, given power in India, that power would be liable to gravitate into the hands of the wealthy Indians.[17]

Maxton was thus opposed to the pure-and-simple nationalism of Gandhi and the Congress Party and gave his backing to the class-based movement centring on the Indian Labour movement.

Although he still retained some informal links with the LAI, expulsion meant that Maxton was free to take part in the LSI congresses. At the 4th Congress in Vienna in July 1931, he articulated the same class analysis of society he had used to qualify his support for Indian independence during a debate on the economic crisis in Germany. Maxton was in a minority when he rejected the views put forward by Otto Bauer of the Austrian Social Democratic Party that the prevention of further gains by Fascists in Germany could only be achieved by the capital-rich countries propping-up the economy through massive injections of economic aid. Maxton argued that it was not the task of the LSI to rescue German Capitalism; on the contrary, it was to hasten its demise and replace it with Socialism. On behalf of the ILP, Maxton asked the German Social Democrats to stop 'acquiesing' in the Bruning government's policies and start fighting in 'earnest against Fascism and Capitalism'. However, for the German Social Democrats there was a world of difference between Bruning-style Capitalism and Hitler's Fascism. Maxton also failed to understand the depth of divisions between the Communist and Socialist movement in Germany, which made a united left-wing stand against the Fascists impossible. Bauer pointed out that the outcome of Maxton's strategy would be civil war and revolution in which the German working class, divided in its loyalties between these parties, would be smashed by its right-wing opponents. However, in many ways Maxton's criticism of the Social Democratic strategy was proven correct. In spite of its defence of parliamentary institutions and collaboration with the Bruning government, the German SPD could not prevent Hitler's rise to power, supported by the very people that Bauer was suggesting Socialists ought to co-operate with. Moreover, after the Dollfuss *coup d'état* in March 1933 and the abortive workers' uprising in February 1934, Bauer admitted in an article, 'Austrian democracy under fire' (1934), that the Weimar-style political manoeuvrings of the Social Democrats had meant the left in Austria was ill-prepared to fight when the crucial moment arrived. From 1931 the ILP had practically nothing to do with the LSI. Although Maxton was overwhelmingly defeated at Vienna, the episode is interesting in terms of his political development in that it shows how committed he was to a revolutionary class position at a time of chronic economic crisis.

4

Maxton's outspoken attacks on Labour's domestic and imperial policies proved to be highly embarrassing to MacDonald as they received wide publicity in the bourgeois press. Consequently, attempts were made to muzzle him. The lead in this strategy was given to Shinwell inside the Commons and Dollan within the ILP. Since 1926 ILP parliamentary group meetings had been badly attended and this had given Maxton and his close associates the opportunity to dictate policy without undue interference. Shinwell sought to end this by deliberately arranging for large attendances at group meetings of those ILP MPs loyal to the MacDonald government. On 19 November 1929 sixty-eight MPs attended a meeting of the parliamentary group to discuss opposition to the second reading of Bondfield's Insurance Bill. A motion supporting the government was carried by 41 to 14 with thirteen abstentions and a further resolution ordering all amendments to government legislation to be passed to the consultative committee of the PLP for vetting was carried by 37 to 3. The decision of the group, even though arrived at by democratic means, could not be accepted by Maxton as it would have effectively meant an end to all criticism of government policy. It would also have meant Maxton submitting to a policy decided upon by MPs who did not share the views of ILP conferences, far less attend them. Failing to carry through this strategy, the PLP on 20 May 1930 re-affirmed its standing orders, which prevented MPs from voting against the government, although the right to abstain was recognised. Moral pressure was applied as, during the stand against the Anomalies Act, a round-robin was signed by over a hundred MPs condemning Maxton's leadership of the ILP.

Dollan supplemented Shinwell's action in the PLP to silence Maxton and other dissident ILPers. At a meeting of the NAC on 7 December 1929 Dollan moved a resolution favouring the calling of a special conference to decide on whether the ILP parliamentary group should offer amendments to government bills. It lost by 3 votes to 10 and a motion moved by Wheatley affirming confidence in Maxton's leadership was carried by the reverse margin. Dollan was more sucessful at the 1930 Scottish ILP

Conference when a motion by Kinning Park ILP expressing approval of the Maxton group's stand against the Insurance Bill was defeated by 93 to 103 votes. The Scottish view, however, was not shared by the other divisional councils who all supported Maxton. At the 1930 ILP Conference Dollan's resolution to refer back the report of the parliamentary group was defeated by a massive majority of 53 to 357 votes, in spite of the fact that it was only the *New Leader* out of all the ILP journals which backed Maxton. The 1930 Conference also called for a restructuring of the ILP parliamentary group which would effectively end all attempts to emasculate the Maxton group in the Commons.

As a result of Conference's decision, the party secretary, John Paton, was instructed to send a letter to all ILP MPs setting out the new terms of membership of the parliamentary group. The most important of these was the one which requested prospective parliamentary candidates to give an undertaking that they would accept in general the policy of the ILP as determined by Annual Conference and, if elected, would be prepared to give effect to it in the Commons. In practice this made the parliamentary group an autonomous body similar to the PLP. The outcome would be that there would be two Labour parties in the Commons. The terms of membership not surprisingly produced a hostile response from the Executive of the Labour Party and from the movement in general. Matters came to a head in a series of by-elections which took place around that time. Candidates who declared their intention of joining the ILP parliamentary group if elected were refused Labour Party endorsement, as in the case of Tom Irwin in the East Renfrewshire by-election of December 1930. The new conditions of membership were, however, rejected by all but eighteen ILP MPs.

Relations between the ILP and the Labour Party reached their nadir after the terms of reference were published. Meetings were initiated between Maxton and Arthur Henderson to find a way out of the impasse and eventually a formula was worked out between the ILP's NAC and the NEC of the Labour Party. The formula recognised the independence of the ILP but also its duties as an organisation affiliated to the Labour Party. It was a conundrum worthy of a Chinese philosopher and, as such, the parties never seemed as though they would resolve their outstanding differences. The negotiations dragged along with Maxton and Henderson both refusing to shift their positions. Unexpectedly, it was the fall of the second Labour government which created the decisive move in the talks and resulted in the ILP disaffiliating itself from the Labour Party.

7 *The fall of the Labour government and disaffiliation*

1

As the world recession deepened and unemployment grew to unprecedented levels in Britain and elsewhere, Labour set its face against radical alternatives to the economic orthodoxy of the Treasury. Balanced budgets, sound money and free trade continued to form the bedrock of government economic policy. The recession showed no signs of bottoming out and an alarmed Labour government in March 1931 set up the May Committee to inquire into the state of the economy. Shortly after this appointment, the financial system was shaken by the collapse in May of the Austrian Credit Ansalt and several banks in Germany; an event which was to enhance the importance of the May Committee.

The response of the German government to the banking failure was to freeze all its foreign assets on 15 July and this effectively transferred the crisis to other money markets, most notably London. The Bank of England was ill-equipped to deal with the crisis; sterling was overvalued and gold reserves were small. Worried overseas investors began withdrawing assets held in London at the rate of £4 million an day, and, with £90 million locked up in Germany, Britain found it difficult to halt the run on its gold reserves. On 28 July loans were secured from New York and Paris and the opportunity to stabilise the situation seemed at hand. However, three days later the May Committee published its alarmist findings, arguing that there would be a budget deficit of £120 million by the end of 1932 if steps were not taken to cut public expenditure. Specifically this meant reducing the pay of government employees and cutting unemployment benefit by as much as twenty per cent.

The report's finding caused another run on the pound and threatened to completely undermine the workings of the gold standard – an article of faith for Labour's Chancellor, Phillip Snowden. To avert this threat, the Bank of England borrowed £50 million from American and French banks. This sum proved insufficient to halt the run on sterling and a further application was made for a second loan of £80 million. It was met by a demand from the New York Federal Reserve Bank that the Labour government, as an act of good faith, carry out the recommendations of the May Committee. The idea of cutting unemployment benefit split the MacDonald Cabinet. To agree to a reduction of the magnitude of twenty per cent would have led to the disaffection of the whole of the Labour movement; not to accept would have meant further runs on the pound and possible bankruptcy. The reliance of MacDonald on conservative advisers and its opposition to any radical economic alternatives to Treasury orthodoxy once again had plunged Labour into a crisis of its own making. Failing, only very narrowly, to convince the Cabinet to accept the total package of economies, which included a ten per cent cut in unemployment benefit, MacDonald and Snowden decided to form a coalition government with the Tories and the Liberals. A General Election soon followed in which Labour was decimated, losing 236 seats, and a national government was elected.

While MacDonald was being kissed by every duchess in London for his actions, the Labour movement cried traitor. To Maxton, MacDonald's conduct was a final proof of the failure of gradualism and a 'complete vindication of the position the ILP had adopted over the last five years'. The following year he wrote in the preface to John Scanlon's book, *The Decline and Fall of the Labour Party*, what he believed to be the fundamental weakness of Labour's approach and what he hoped might result from the government's fall, saying:

> To me their failure was due to a complete lack of faith in Socialism. . . and their lack of belief in. . . the working classes to achieve Socialism. . . I firmly believe that out of the defeat that at present faces the working classes in their effort for Socialist liberation, out of the schism and faction will develop speedily a new political Socialist movement of the working class which will be strong enough in faith, in morale and in personnel to achieve success where its predecessors failed.

Maxton also strongly asserted that finance capital was culpable in the fall of the Labour government and that it, and not the government, was the real power in the country. The need to bring financial institutions to heel was a pressing concern for the Labour movement, he argued, if such an event was not to happen again.

The official Labour leaders did not so much blame the actions of MacDonald and Snowden for the débâcle of 1931, rather they chose to single out Maxton and the other ILP dissidents. By attacking those associated with Maxtonite attacks on the second Labour government, official Labour could avoid taking the difficult road of tough self-examination. Arthur Woodburn, Secretary of the Scottish Labour Party, accused Maxton of conducting anti-Labour propaganda which 'confused our own people and weakened their enthusiasm'.[18] A survey carried out by *Forward* of Scottish constituencies into reasons for Labour's miserable electoral performance saw the oppositionalism of the Maxton group to the policies of the previous Labour government invoked as one of the major factors. That defeat saw the differences between the ILP and the Labour Party brought to a head. The question this time, however, was not under what conditions the ILP would remain affiliated to the Labour Party but for how long.

2

On the surface the disagreement between the parties was procedural rather than ideological. What Maxton demanded was the rescinding of Labour's standing orders, as in their present form they prevented MPs from voting against a Labour government on political grounds. To accept them was effectively to put an end to criticisms within the PLP. For the Labour Party, the issue centred on party discipline. The Executive demanded that an affiliated organisation should cease to act as an autonomous body and adhere to party standing orders. In practice, this meant that the ILP had to withdraw its terms of membership of the parliamentary group but in many ways the procedural issue was a specious one, as the question of voting freedom would hardly have loomed large in the reconvened parliament with Labour in a minority position. Maxton and the Labour MPs would have been united in their attacks on the policies of the national government, particularly over the treatment of the unemployed. Thus the issue of independence was symptomatic of a much deeper division within the Labour movement.

In spite of this, the debate within the ILP tended to revolve almost exclusively around the right of MPs to criticise and vote against a Labour government. Three distinct groupings emerged: the affiliationists, who included E. F. Wise and Dollan, the conditional affiliationists, who included Kirkwood, and the disaffiliationists, who included Maxton, Brockway and the Revolutionary Policy Committee (RPC). The first group accepted Labour's standing orders unconditionally, for the simple reason that outside the mainstream Labour movement the ILP would rapidly disintegrate as a political force, while the conditionalists advocated continued negotiations in hope that some sort of compromise would be reached with Labour. Maxton and the rest of the ILP argued that the fight for SIOT could be carried on more effectively outside the Labour Party as the ILP would not be restricted in its activity and propaganda by standing orders. As far as Maxton was concerned, staying in the Labour Party meant 'creating in the public mind that the capitalist system in all its essentials must be preserved at all costs'.

The first national conference to decide the question was held in March 1932. Prior to this, disaffiliation had been defeated at the Scottish ILP conference in January. After defeat in Glasgow, Maxton let it be known to the press that if the result was repeated in Blackpool he and some other ILP MPs would resign. This may have put extra pressure on the delegates but it did not significantly influence the outcome of the Blackpool Conference. The vote went in favour of conditional affiliation by 250 to 33 votes, with disaffiliation being lost by 144 to 183. Following the Conference, negotiations were once more resumed with the Labour Party.

A deputation of Brockway (Chairman), Jowett (Treasurer), Maxton, Dollan, Stephen and Wallhead met members of Labour's NEC. The talks soon reached an impasse over the latter's refusal to accept any amendments to standing orders until the ILP had agreed to them as a basis of affilation. The negotiations broke down over this issue and the NAC had no option but to recommend disaffiliation to the membership. A special conference was called in July 1932 to discuss the NAC's recommendations. Ironically it was held in the city where the ILP had been formed thirty-nine years previously – Bradford. Dollan and Kirkwood put the case for affiliation, but it was Maxton who triumphed. He argued simply that the 'Labour Party were not prepared to allow the ILP to abide by its principles' and to remain in the party would reduce ILPers to 'docile supporters of whatever the wider movement desired'. Unconditional affiliation was defeated by 142 to 241 votes and disaffiliation carried by a large majority. This in effect meant a 'clean break' from the official Labour movement as the RPC had tagged onto the original resolution the immediate withdrawal of all ILP members from positions of authority and responsibility in the Co-operative movement, the Labour Party and the trades unions, as well as opting out of paying the political levy through the latter to Labour.

Brockway's announcement of disaffiliation was greeted with spontaneous cheering and a burst of the *Red Flag*. The affiliationists went off to found their own organisation; in Scotland, Dollan, Johnston and other sympathisers founded the Scottish Socialist Party; in England, former ILPers under the leadership of Stafford Cripps launched the Socialist League and both were affiliated to the Labour Party. Maxton addressed the delegates in his usual optimistic manner, declaring: 'I shall try to get a Parliamentary majority for the ILP within five years. But I shall try also within these five years to unite the working classes without any imposition from above by non-socialists. I shall make it a real unity of revolutionary socialist forces.'

3

Historians and others have generally given the thumbs down to Maxton's decision to lead the ILP out of the Labour Party. Their responses have varied between anger and incredulity. Keith Middlemas in *The Clydesiders* (1965) spoke of the decision as an act of suicide during a temporary fit of insanity, G. D. H. Cole in *A History of the Labour Party from 1914* (1948) put it down to the premature death of John Wheatley, Emanuel Shinwell in *Conflict Without Malice* (1955) put it down to Maxton's lack of application, as did David Marquand in *Ramsay MacDonald*, while Colin Cross in *Phillip Snowden* (1966) saw his excessive sentimentality as the main reason. The overriding impression conveyed is one of a man out of touch with political reality, whose intellectual indolence led him to fall under the influence of sinister conspirators grouped around the RPC but who might have been saved from committing political suicide had the shrewder and wiser Wheatley lived longer. Remaining within a divided and demoralised Labour Party, Maxton would have been a possible candidate for the leadership – a view expressed by Shinwell, Ellen Wilkinson, Labour MP for Jarrow, and strangely enough by Beaverbrook, who wrote in November 1931 to Maxton, saying: '[although] Your policy doesn't suit me. . . as we must have an opposition I'm sure you won't mind if I rejoice that you are the real leader of it.'[19] The major problem with this interpretation is that it is deeply flawed at a fundamental level. It fails to come to terms with Maxton's driving idealism and his critique of a Capitalist society in crisis, his relationsip with Wheatley and his role in the Labour movement as perceived by him and by those in authority.

There is little doubt that Maxton did rely on Wheatley for political advice; indeed he once claimed: 'John is my leader, I follow John'. However, as stated earlier, it was a complementary partnership between the orator and the tactician in which Maxton was no junior partner. As the Cook/Maxton manifesto campaign showed, he was not Wheatley's poodle. Their relationship is made clear in an off-the-cuff remark recorded by John Scanlon, in which Maxton said to Wheately, 'You will find me the trickiest leader you ever tried to lead.'[20] It was Wheatley's task to devise the strategy and tactics and to detail the political programme; it was Maxton's to win popularity for it and to expound its general principles to the working class. Furthermore, there is no reason to believe that, had Wheatley not died in May 1930, he would have opposed disaffiliation. From 1926 onwards the political and philosophical direction of Wheatley was towards disaffiliation. Samuel Cooper, in his unpublished study of Wheatley, shares this view when he concludes that the death of Wheatley 'brought no noticeable change in the behaviour of the ILP in Parliament'.[21] Maxton's leadership was not the vital factor, rather it was the integration of the Labour Party into mainstream party politics which led to disaffiliation.

Maxton's laziness is a debatable point. His energy and commitment to advancing ILP policy in the Commons and on platforms throughout Britain is indisputable. There is, however, a more credible case to be made out for intellectual indolence. Apart from a cursory study of Marx undertaken at university, Maxton showed no sustained appetite for political or Socialist theory. The best that can be said is that he dabbled in rather than delved into Marxist/Socialist writing. This fact helps to explain his contradictory poistion on a number of issues. For example, he supported the moderate Keynesian programme SIOT and at the same time subscribed to the revolutionary class-war position of the Cook/Maxton manifesto; he advocated the establishment of Socialism as an act of free-willed men and women and yet his belief, as we shall see, in the collapse of Capitalism was a negation of this view as it implied that human actions were determined by impersonal economic forces. Undoubtedly Maxton's lack of theory laid him open to manipulation from those with a firmer grip on dialectics, especially Brockway and the RPC, but the argument is circular. If Maxton was so easily manipulated why did the left succeed where the right failed? The manipulation thesis is not only offensive to Maxton, it also fails to appreciate his analysis of the Labour Party and its role in the Capitalist system – a system which Maxton increasingly saw as one in terminal and irreversible decline.

Maxton thought that the collapse of Capitalism was imminent. Writing in the *New Leader* (September 1931), he stated that he saw no end to the present crisis other than 'complete catastrophe' and claimed that there were 'now only months, and shortly there will only be weeks' before it arrived. The crisis was analysed by Maxton in classic Marxist terms as one generated by overproduction. The basic contradiction between the power to produce and the limited power to consume was vividly displayed on a global scale. World markets were glutted and, as a result, people stood idle and hungry in the face of a mountain of wealth. This was a harsh reminder of the class ownership of the means of production. Maxton fully expected the crisis to radicalise the working class, declaring in a speech at the Colliseum Theatre in Glasgow on 21 April 1932 that 'the economic conditions that the people are experiencing, are teaching them at a rate, at a speed and in a way, a revolutionary conception that no amount of oratory, no amount of persuasion could ever get into their minds'.[22] It was the task of Socialists, Maxton argued, to develop an organisation which would guide the revolutionary potential of the masses in the direction of Socialism. The Labour Party with its reformism and commitment to parliamentarianism was incapable of giving the workers the right lead, hence the need for a new party based on democratic principles and the class struggle. By remaining in the Labour Party, Maxton saw himself as containing working-class radicalism rather than giving expression and a lead to it. Thus it was his belief in the collapse of Capitalism and the consciousness which flowed from it which constituted the real reason for Maxton's decision to support disaffiliation. G. D. H. Cole caught the essence of Maxton's mood when he wrote:

> Maxton, coming from Clydeside and conscious of the rising temper of the workers there and in other depressed areas as they felt the weight of the Means Test and of other measures of economy and repression, probably took the Labour Party's election defeat to mean more than it turned out to mean, and had hopes of building up the ILP into a mass party standing for a left wing policy.[23]

However sincere in his views, it remains true that Maxton's

analysis of the economic crisis and its effect on the balance of class forces in society was flawed both theoretically and empirically. His Crisis-Socialism neglected the fundamental question of class consciousness and the capacity of Capitalism to stagger from one economic crisis to another. Predicting the end of Capitalism was a Socialist pastime dating back to the late nineteenth century. Maxton himself had stated in the mid-1920s that 'Capitalism was now on the verge of collapse' and could no longer be 'saved by repairs and patchwork'. If, indeed, a causal link existed between rapidly deteriorating economic conditions and revolutionary class consciousness then it would have been in the interests of Socialists to work at worsening the living standards of the workers. There is, and was, no automatic link between poverty and class consciousness. Moreover, an economic crisis is rarely total as within decaying forms of capital accumulation emerge new areas of economic growth. In Britain in the 1930s the emergence of the motor car, the radio and civilian aircraft industries laid the basis of revitalised output. Workers associated with the new manufacturing industries and those in the south east corner of England were enjoying rising standards of living, while those in the depressed north suffered mass unemployment and poverty. The working class of the north may have joined in the occasional hunger march, but, on the whole, they sat out the depression in sullen resentment waiting, like the politicians, for the expected upturn in trade. The very fact that they had voted in the national government in 1931 with 556 seats and seventy per cent of the popular vote demonstrated the extent to which Maxton had misjudged the mood of the workers. Finally, the failure of the CPGB to increase its membership beyond 2,500 at this time was an obvious indication that the working class was anything like radicalised.

In spite of the questionable optimism behind disaffiliation, remaining in the Labour party was a no-win situation for Maxton.

Given Labour's insistence that the Maxton group adhere to standing orders, the best that could have been hoped for in the long run was something akin to the status of the present day Tribune group. Distinctive maybe, but hardly independent. Outside of the Labour Party Maxton saw the ILP performing the same role as the former did during the lifetime of the last Liberal government. In the years 1906-12 Labour had no hope of winning office and yet it had pressurised the Liberals into introducing a remarkable package of social legislation. Although the reality behind the Liberal reforms was more complex than Maxton was prepared to admit, the important thing to grasp is that to him numbers were not the final arbiters of progressive political and social change; organisation and mobilisation of the workers were just as important. The latter was a role that Maxton felt, in the absence of Socialism, the ILP could clearly play.

The idea that, by staying in the Labour Party, his role could have become more decisive is fanciful. Maxton had not the remotest chance of becoming party leader as the key to that was held in the hands of the trades union leaders. After 1931 they had become the real power brokers in the Labour Party and with over fifty per cent of the seats on the National Council of Labour they also determined the parameters of party policy. Any serious contender for the leadership of the party would have to have swung over the trades unions and in Maxton's case this was highly unlikely. His record of criticism of, and opposition to, trades union officialdom, established during the Cook/Maxton manifesto campaign assured him of the lasting enmity of this section of the Labour movement. Labour, under the control of the TUC and, in particular, Ernest Bevin, was a conformist, socially moderate party, and Maxton's championship of militantly Socialist policies made him appear as a wild-eyed dreamer to the former. As David Kirkwood pointed out in *My Life of Revolt*: 'the trades union members are afraid lest he leads them in paths where they do not care to tread.'

Another aspect of this question of lost opportunity put forward by the left-wing historians is that Maxton's departure allowed the Labour Party to become dominated by the centre right and, in the process, destroyed the radical missionary zeal of the party. The former radical heartlands of the ILP, like Glasgow, the West Riding and Lancashire, gave way to the machine politics of the 1930s and beyond. By the time of the revival of the Labour left in the 1950s these areas had little to contribute.[24] This thesis is open to criticism; firstly, the Labour Party was already under the domination of the centre right prior to disaffiliation and with the greater trades union involvement in the 1930s the right's power would have become more entrenched and, secondly, areas such as Clydeside and Yorkshire opposed disaffiliation and were under the control of machine politicians like Dollan. It is unlikely that the history of the Labour Party would have been written any differently for Maxton's continued membership of it.

However, there is little denying that the price of disaffiliation was a high one for the ILP. Although Maxton spurned the suggestion by the *Daily Herald* that he was leading the ILP into the political wilderness, claiming that 'in the months immediately in front of us the people in this country will develop a temper about political affairs such as has never been demonstrated since the days of Cromwell', the converse proved to be true. The 1931 General Election had seen ILP representation in the Commons slump to a point where disaffiliation reduced the numbers to three. Membership was also falling badly. In the period July–November 1932 it fell by around fifty per cent, with the loss of 203 branches out of a total of 653. The worst losses were in Scotland where 128 branches resigned but there were also important fall-offs in such strongholds as Lancashire and Yorkshire. Loss of members inevitably led to falling income. In 1934 grants to divisional councils were cut and this, in turn, led in the next year to the cessation of grants for the employment of full-time divisional organisers. Following disaffiliation the party also became more London-based, out of touch with the aspirations of the workers of the industrial north and more under the influence of the RPC.

The blame for this serious decline has been placed on Maxton's shoulders. But in many ways this is a highly suspect misreading of the history of the ILP. As Dowse shows, the ILP was a dwindling force in terms of influence and membership before Maxton became chairman in 1926. The reason, as Marwick points out, lies in the emergence of the Labour Party as a monolithic mass party, which meant there was less room for an autonomous organisation like the ILP.[25] Most of the ILPers, especially the ambitious, recognised this and dropped their dual membership. What Maxton did was to accelerate this decline; he was not resposible for or culpable of originating it. However, there is a danger in interpreting the decline of the ILP solely in terms of numbers and political power. These things are important, indeed crucial, to any party but the impact of a political organisation can be expressed and experienced in other ways. The 1930s were to prove to be a fascinating period in Maxton's political development as he struggled with the problems of leading a small party which, although larger than the CPGB, faced the prospect of marginalisation and the task of developing a form of Socialism free from Social Democratic and Stalinist defects in the socially and politically devastating atmosphere of Fascism, unemployment and war.

8 The first United Front

1

Following the débâcle of 1931, disaffiliation and the adoption of the 'clean break' policy by the ILP, the British Labour movment was demoralised and divided. Yet the challenges it faced had grown substantially. The early 1930s saw the election of a right-wing national government committed to cutting public expenditure in the midst of mass unemployment and human despair. In Europe there was the rise of Fascism and the military adventurism associated with it which threatened to plunge the world once more into war. There was also the Fascist challenge to be met in Britain with the emergence of the British Union of Fascists (BUF) under the leadership of the former Labour MP Oswald Mosley. In this conflict-charged atmosphere Maxton began to experiment with various political forms and strategies and, in consequence, his politics became more firmly rooted in the Marxist concept of the class struggle. The most vital need for the Labour movement, he argued, was the establishment of workers' power as an immediate and practical proposition. Failure to achieve this would lead to economic and social catastrophe on a global scale. And, while Maxton's siren call would generally fall on deaf ears, his response to those imminent dangers were to prove that the early 1930s would be one of the most fertile and interesting periods of his political development.

2

Maxton's acceptance of the concept of class struggle provided him with a theoretical framework in which to analyse human activity. This was fruitfully extended to the sphere of education. His formerly progressive reformist critique of education, which relied heavily on the human capital argument, broadened into a Marxist analysis of the bourgeois educational system, especially at the higher levels. In December 1930 Maxton turned down an offer of an honorary LL.D made to him by J. M. Barrie, playwright and then Chancellor of the University of Edinburgh, because as 'a Socialist. . . I feel that anything that tends to mark out a man from other men should not be acceptable'.[26] In Maxton's view, education not only had to be democratic, but it also had to be geared towards the political emancipation of the working class. In his analysis the universities were an indivisible part of the Capitalist system and therefore, anti-working class. Socialists had to build counter-educational agencies aimed at developing class awareness among workers and, ultimately, the overthrow of capitalism. Once the latter had been achieved then education would be experienced as a liberating force and not as something designed to meet the needs of the Capitalist labour market.

Maxton outlined his complete educational (and political) philosophy in his short monograph, *If I Were A Dictator* (1935). In a system of Socialist education there would be a three-tier structure of primary, secondary and higher education. At the primary level, schooling was to begin at eight years of age. The schools were to be set in tasteful surroundings with large expanses of grass, animals and trees. There were also to be sporting facilities available like swimming pools, gymnasiums, playing fields and so on. The maximum number of pupils on the class roll was to be twenty-five, attending for four hours a day, five days a week. Although the curriculum provided for the mastery of the 3Rs within the first three years, basic education was to be mixed with subjects intended to lead the child towards a rudimentary understanding of the natural and physical sciences and to develop the human personality through a variety of activities which included singing, dancing, drama and games. The accent was to be on co-operation with no examinations. However, pupils were expected to reach defined standards of competency in a chosen range of subjects.

Secondary education was to involve the teaching of mathematics, science and social skills at both the level of theory and practice. Subjects like history, geography and citizenship were to be conveyed through the medium of discussion between teachers and pupils. Between the ages of fifteen and eighteen the pupils were to spend three-quarters of their time in education and a quarter in work, thus establishing a basis for the abolition of the division of mental and manual labour. Advanced education would be made available to all and each person would be expected to take a course in higher education. But, as in school, study and work would continue to co-exist. The courses were to be broadly similar to those already taught within existing institutions of higher education with one notable exception; language schools were to be made redundant as there would be one world language. The centres of excellence, where the main research and development projects would be undertaken, would be international with entry restricted to those who had given proof of their ability and active interest. For those who wished to opt out of the state system on ethical or religious grounds, allowances would be made as long as their aims were 'communal and their motives good'. The anti-authoritarian and democratic nature of Maxton's educational philosophy contrasted sharply with prevailing educational practices which emphasised rote learning and obedience. It was also clear that Maxton was thinking of Socialism as a world-wide system of society; a development which was out of sympathy with the Stalinist trend towards Socialism in one country. However, his views on education were not entirely free from elitist leanings, as his centres of excellence inevitably involved some form of screening of candidates and higher resource inputs vis-à-vis other forms of education.

The vision of education Maxton developed was essentially a reaction to his own experiences as a teacher in Glasgow; the role he assigned education in the process of political change was something which emerged out of the socio-economic conditions of the late 20s and early 30s. Education and propaganda had been the main catalysts of change for Maxton but during the economic crisis he came to the conclusion that class struggle held primacy in developing class consciousness. As the market system was in the throes of irreversible collapse new forms and new ideas of struggle, of which education could only form a part, had to be utilised if workers' power was to be realised. Past political practice had to be revised to meet changing circumstances and this involved a reformulation of the traditional roles ascribed by the Labour movement to education and parliamentary politics in bringing about Socialism.

3

Maxton's disillusionment with purely parliamentary reforms of political action had been evident from the publication of the Cook/Maxton manifesto of 1928. However, after 1932 his criticism became more strident and his impatience greater. At the Scottish ILP Conference in January 1933, he stated that the moment would soon arrive when the British workers would say to the institutions of parliament 'Get out the way'. In an article a few months later in the *New Leader* (21 April) Maxton returned once more to the inadequacies of the parliamentary system, claiming that it was the task of the ILP to disabuse the workers of the idea that 'Parliament alone would bring about the establishment of a Socialist state'. Maxton argued that the Labour movement in the past had placed too much stress on electoral politics as the instrument of social change and not enough on trades unions and co-operative societies. This might have put him at odds with the 'clean break' policy adopted at Bradford in 1932 but Maxton was never enthusiastic about isolation from the mainstream Labour movement. What was needed, he argued, was a united struggle conducted on all fronts, centred on the dual power concept of parliament and workers' councils as had existed in Russia prior to, and immediately after, the 1917 October Revolution.

The inspiration behind the idea of dual power may have come from his highly sympathetic study of *Lenin* published in 1932. The research involved allowed Maxton to examine in some depth political ideas and forms initiated during a period of great upheaval. From his study he may have come to the conclusion that, in the similar conditions in which Britain found itself in the early 1930s, workers' councils could be a better way of combating unemployment and Fascism than pure and simple parliamentarianism. Indeed, the political realities of Labour's position made such a direction for Maxton almost inevitable. The General Election of 1931 had reduced Labour's representation in the Commons to such an extent that it was incapable of articulating the interests of the working class in any meaningful sense. The only value of parliamentary institutions to the Labour movement was in providing a platform on which to score propaganda points against government policies. At the same time as it was politically powerless, the Labour movement had to face the threat of Fascism and the reality of mass unemployment. New circumstances, therefore, called for new strategies. The struggle for Socialism had to be conducted on all fronts, including the non-industrial community-based forms of action. Such a strategy was more easily controlled by extra-parliamentary bodies, hence the need for workers' councils.

The purpose and structure of the councils were laid out in a pamphlet, *A Clear Lead* (1933), written jointly by Brockway and Maxton. The council movement was to include all the revolutionary sections of the working class; that is, the CPGB and the ILP, organisations of the unemployed like the National Unemployed Workers Movement (NUWM), factory, mine and workshop committees based on industrial rather than craft or occupational lines, as well as estate committees and tenants' defence associations. These bodies, while still enjoying the right to autonomy and independence in the running of their affairs and in deciding on policy, would be linked through a national committee. *A Clear Lead* demonstrated how far Maxton and the ILP had come under the influence of Leninism. It was around this time that the *New Leader* began publishing articles from Trotsky and Maxton managed to obtain a temporary residence permit for the former in the Channel Islands. These events appear to have been more than coincidence.

To effect the new political direction, the ILP made overtures to other parties and groups on the left, although it was only the Communists who expressed a willingness to co-operate. The CPGB had been eager to build alliances with other left-wing parties against Fascism since the abandonment of the Comintern's disastrous 'class against class' strategy. As early as October 1931 Maxton himself had been exhorting the two parties to lay aside their differences and divise 'common tactics, common programmes [and] a common platform'. However, the real step towards unity took place in Sheffield in December 1932 when the activists there organised a week-end conference on the theme of working-class militancy and unity. At the conference were 150 representatives of the ILP, CPGB, trades unions, co-operative guilds and the young Communist League of Youth. Maxton was accorded an ecstatic reception by the delegates when he spoke on the need for united action by the workers as the only way out of the contemporary crisis.

The outcome of the conference was the setting up of a Sheffield Workers' Council of Action with members from each of the organisations present. Although Maxton had to defend himself from Communist attacks in subsequent issues of the *New Leader*, the Sheffield conference marked the beginning of the United Front in Britain. The rise of Hitler to power in Germany, partly as a result of the historic divisions between Socialists and Communists, further strengthened the idea of unity of the left, as well as making it more urgent. Maxton, in the *New Leader* (3 February 1933), blamed the German left for failing to unite against the Fascist threat and concluded: 'It is now to be hoped that a common danger will now produce the unity that a working class analysis of the situation should have provided before. . . other workers' movements in other lands still have time to learn and act.'

In March 1933 the CPGB approached the Labour party, TUC and ILP with a proposal to form a United Front against unemployment and Fascism. The official Labour leadership predictably turned down the Communist offer but the ILP was responsive. An agreement was reached between the ILP and the Communists and this was also extended to the Socialist League (SL). The SL had been set up by Labour members to perform the same role as the ILP had previously done in the Labour movement and contained within its ranks such outstanding personalities as Stafford Crips, Aneurin Bevan and E. F. Wise. The agreement allowed each organisation to retain its independece and, at the same time, co-operate over a wide range of issues of common concern such as the means test, hunger marches, anti-Fascism, anti-war and other day-to-day issues. However, the United Front was soon in troubled waters and co-operation proved short-lived. Part of the problem was the hostile reaction of the official Labour movement to its activities. The trades unions opposed the idea of workers' councils because they threatened to undermine their authority, as had the Communist-inspired Minority Movement a few years previously. The Labour Party had always stood out against Communist affiliation to it and this position hardened during the Communists' 'Social Fascist' campaign. The campaign was also directed at the ILP. Herbert Morrison, on behalf of Labour's NEC, wrote a pamphlet entitled *Democracy and Dictatorship*, which called on workers to fight through Labour 'against dictators, Fascist or Communist'.

The other problem was the CPGB itself. Its strategy was directed towards the eventual assimilation of the ILP and to achieve this it adopted the classic entryist technique of 'boring from within'. The instrument chosen for taking over the ILP was the RPC, whose leading lights were Jack Gaster and Dr C. K. Cullen. The RPC had emerged in 1931 during the disaffiliation crisis as representative of opinion in a number of London branches. Its influence had increased after 1932 owing to the ILP becoming more London-based. Gaster and Cullen wished to win the ILP over to membership of Comintern and to this end succeeded in convincing the party to enter into negotiations with the latter regarding conditions of membership. The grander ambition was to see the ILP merge with the CPGB. Until talks opened with Comintern, Maxton was very tolerant of the RPC's activities, perhaps because he was not aware of their real intentions or because he did not fully understand their tactics. However, once discussions were in progress with the Comintern he became opposed to the idea of any sort of affiliation.

Maxton, although an admirer of the Soviet Union, was by no means uncritical. At the ILP conference in April 1930 he may have claimed that the 'most important political happening in the world at the moment is the Russian Five Year Plan' but he was not fooled, as the Webbs were, into believing that the USSR was some kind of Socialist Utopia. In *Lenin* he wrote: 'It is not yet posssible to say that Russia has in practice realised the Utopian state of plenty, of liberty, and of happiness, nor is it possible to say that other countries may not reach a better state in speedier and less harsh ways.'

In 1934 Maxton became even more antagonistic to the Soviet Union when it entered the League of Nations – Lenin's 'thieves' kitchen'. He argued at a meeting of the NAC of the ILP that the 'Russian Government cannot become allied with the French Government without subduing the class struggle previously carried out by the French Communists. It cannot seek alliance with the British Government without moderating the class struggle carried on by the oppressed colonial peoples against both British and French imperialism.'

The more open the criticism of the USSR in the ILP, the weaker the position of the RPC became. This tendency was buttressed by two other factors; firstly, the desire of the CPBG to work with all 'progressive' forces against Fascism and to fight for the return of a Labour government in the 1935 General Election, instead of building a revolutionary working-class movement and, secondly, the publishing of the findings of a party poll on the question of continued co-operation with the Communists. Around two-thirds of the active membership of the ILP were opposed to working with the CPGB and this made the RPC's strategy more or less redundant. At an NAC meeting in early February 1934, Maxton and a majority of the Council voted against an attempt by Gaster to commit the party to closer links with the CPGB with a view to building 'one United Revolutionary Party'. When Conference met, a resolution sponsored by the RPC calling for 'sympathetic affiliation with Comintern and continued collaboration with the Communist Party' was defeated by a large majority. Gaster and the other leading members of the RPC resigned from the ILP and returned to, or joined, the

CPGB. At the same conference the 'clean break' policy was overturned, allowing for the re-establishment of ties with the Labour movement, and Maxton was once again elected Chairman of the party.

This disastrous end to what had been one of the most imaginative political intiatives of the early 1930's should not disguise the fact that the brief relationship was not entirely unfruitful. Most notably, it publicised the plight of the unemployed. The NUWM with the help of the CPGB and the ILP organised a series of hunger marches aimed at shaking the complacency of the middle classes and pushing the government into doing something about the unemployed. In January/February 1934 one of the largest marches set out to bring the unemployed protest to London. Although physically incapable of leading the march, Maxton was instrumental in getting the Commons to debate the issue of unemployment and in getting a delegation of the marchers admitted to Downing Street, where MacDonald refused to see them. On 27 February the Prime Minister had written to Maxton stating that he would 'be very glad' to see him 'though not with them', that is, the unmemployed. Indeed, in the Commons it was Maxton who led the fight against the reactionary social policies of the national government in the absence of a strong and determined official opposition. Journalists tended to descibe the small Maxton clique and not the Labour Party as the 'official opposition' and Maxton himself through his 'skilful and persistent manoeuvring and first class contribution to debate' as 'the leader of a Party'.[27]

There was also the campaign against Mosley's BUF, which intensified after the notorious Olympia meeting of June 1934. The emergence of Fascism was not a phenomenon Maxton saw as restricted to Europe; rather it was an automatic response of the ruling classes to deep-seated crisis in the Capitalist system. Already he had detected signs of moves towards the erection of a corporate state in Britain. Addressing an ILP summer school two months after the Olympia meeting, Maxton attacked the close co-operation of leading industrialists and trades union leaders evident since the Mond/Turner talks of 1927-8, saying 'the Trades Unions are tending to work themselves into the fabric of the capitalist state. . . they are finding a community of interests with the employers in their own industries rather than with the workers of other industries. That is a Fascist tendency'.[28] The policing policies of the national government also seemed to point to the undermining of democracy and the suppression of dissent. The re-organisation of the Metropolitan Police and the setting up of a staff college were interpreted by Maxton as 'designed for the suppression of the workers' by placing in command of the police 'men of the same class as the present government'.

Therefore, although the United Front achieved very little of practical value, it was able to highlight and publicise issues of fundamental importance connected with unemployment and the nature of Fascism. That the political experiment was transient was the result of a number of factors, not the least being the hostility of the official Labour movement and the machinations of the Communists. The belief in Labour unity, however, was not totally extinguished. As Fascism and war became a more tangible threat in the late 1930s, it revived itself. As for Maxton himself, this period was a remarkable one in terms of his political evolution. The early 1930s demonstrated how far his adherence to Marxist ideology had increased. The years also showed his capacity for leadership, not only for his skill in debate and political manoeuvre in the Commons, but also in his handling of the RPC challenge. As the storm clouds over Europe increasingly darkened, the closing years of the decade would test these qualities to the full.

9   *Dress rehearsal*

1

The General Election of 1935 brought little indication that unemployment and the rise of Fascism had done much to radicalise the British working class to any great extent. The Labour Party increased its representation in the Commons to 154 seats but the Tory-dominated national government with 413 seats retained a massive majority. The ILP, although winning only four seats, put up a reasonable performance considering that it faced opposition from accredited Labour candidates. Maxton himself amost doubled his majority in Bridgeton. His victory was made all the sweeter by the fact that he had his new wife to share it with. On 14 March he had married his private secretary, Madeline Glasier, in a quiet ceremony at Battersea Registry Office. He had known Madeline since 1923 when she was Secretary of the University Labour Party at the London School of Economics. So impressed was she with Maxton's oratory and Socialist vision that she offered to become his honorary (unpaid) private secretary. Friendship eventually blossomed into love and the couple enjoyed a close and harmonious relationsip until Maxton's death in 1946. The election itself was fought out mainly on the issues of foreign policy. The Labour Party campaigned on its policy of peace through the League of Nations' idea of collective security. This policy had already been put to the test in the Abyssinian War but in the following year it was put even more severely under pressure. 1936 witnessed the re-occupation of the Rhineland by Hitler and the beginning of the Spanish Civil War. Maxton's reactions to these important events can only be understood within the terms of his overall Socialist philosophy which, since 1928, had hardened into a rather idiosyncratic Marxist analysis of society.

Maxton's Socialist philosophy was mapped out in his short book *If I Was A Dictator* (1935). His vision of Socialism was not one confined to national frontiers, rather it was a world-wide system of society based on the common ownership and democratic control of the means of production, distribution and (in the short term) exchange. In the changed context of social relationships Maxton envisaged that money, as a surface reflection of the unsocial ownership of wealth, would gradually disappear as the principle of distribution on the basis of need took hold and common ownership of wealth became entrenched in society. However, as long as people needed Capitalist incentives to work then money would have to be retained. Socialist society could only move as fast and as far as people wished if individual freedom was not to be endangered. Social coercion was not part of Maxton's humanistic vision of society. Before this ideal society could be introduced, workers had to take into public ownership the land, mines, transport and banks, not only to give them experience in running society but also to improve their standard of living by placing purchasing power in their own hands. Although this was similar to the reformist SIOT programme, Maxton's Socialism saw the former as a means to an end and not, as in the 1920s, as an end in itself. This process of socialisation was seen by him as occurring more or less simultaneously throughout the advanced industrial nations. Once the workers, imbued with revolutionary spirit, had won power then within 'two months', Maxton argued, a 'world public service organisation' would be in a position to re-organise 'commerce, finance, agriculture, and industry on the most economic basis as far as human labour is concerned'.

His views were broadly in line with classical Socialist thinkers such as Engels, Marx and William Morris but, on the whole, could be considered more Utopian. Maxton, like Robert Owen before him, imagined that the ruling classes were rational and enlightened and could be expected, therefore, to place their intellects and abilities at the disposal of any movement or society which displayed similar characteristics. Thus in a radio debate in 1929, subsequently published under the title of *The Case of Benn v. Maxton*, he argued that 'all the most responsible figures in world commerce today would give their services unstintingly under the new conditions'. Furthermore, many of his ideas on running industry in a Socialist society were based on the assumption that the Capitalist managerial structure could be successfully transferred from one sociey to the other. This was a practical impossibility given the authoritarian and hierarchical nature of managerial structures in a Capitalist economy. The values of democratic control and free co-operation associated with Socialism would have necessitated the re-structuring of the management of resources. In spite of his Utopianism, Maxton's world view of Socialism meant that the problems thrown up by Capitalism were analysed with an international rather than national perspective. This was important in determining his attitude to the series of conflicts which emerged around this time as a result of Fascist expansionism.

2

A few months before the General Election of 1935, Italy invaded Abyssinia (Ethiopia); an act condemned by the League of Nations. In Britain the Labour Party called on the League to impose international sanctions against the Italians. The ILP took a different approach as they saw the League, in the words of Maxton, as 'a fraud, an imposter. . . a propaganda body passing resolutions without any power to put them into operation'.[29] Moreover, the real purpose of the League to the ILP was to preserve the imperial territories of Britain and France and to suppress revolutionary movements. Thus, to support sanctions against Italy imposed by the League of Nations was to ally oneself with the imperialist powers and the status quo. This led the ILP to call for working-class sanctions against the aggressor, including a ban on the handling of armament shipments to Italy and the transportation of Italian troops to Africa.

This was in agreement with the view put forward by the International Centre of Revolutionary Socialist Parties to which the ILP was affiliated. As a result, a campaign was launched in the *New Leader* to rally the ILP members to the policy. However, the party's Inner Executive (Maxton, Brockway, McGovern, Stephen and Alpin) came to the opposing view that working-class sanctions were in practice indistinguishable from the League's sanctions and that it was not a war in which workers should take sides. As Maxton put it, 'to support sanctions or the threat of sanctions. . . was tantamount to a declaration that there were serious differences – for a Socialist – between the two sides. It was not a matter of support or non-support, of assessing praise or blame, since the struggle was between two rival dictators.'[30] Maxton went on to argue in the Commons in April 1936 that if sanctions had not been applied by the League and if the Abyssinian people had not been misled into thinking that they would have brought Italy to its knees, then the native population would have ceased fighting, accepted their fate and thousands of lives would have been saved. This view was attacked by Hugh Dalton, later Chancellor of the Exchequer in the 1945 Labour government, who remarked that the repeal of oil sanctions would have allowed the Italian bomber pilots to intensify the killing and destruction in Abyssinia. Maxton retorted that partial sanctions against war were not enough, the only solution was to impose sanctions on all conditions and materials of war. His reply not only failed to convince the Commons, it also opened him to attack from his critics within the ILP.

Maxton's position on the Abyssinian War was criticised at the ILP's Keighley Conference in April 1936. A resolution moved by C. L. R. James, black Socialist and author, condemning the Inner Executive's line and calling on the ILP to support him as a black worker in his fight for freedom for the peoples of Abyssinia was accepted by the Conference on a vote of 70 to 57. Maxton and his fellow ILP MPs refused to stand by the decision, arguing that, as they had stood as anti-war candidates at the last General Election, they could not support a policy which placed the ILP on a pro-war footing. Maxton offered his resignation as Chairman of the party and this forced Conference, after some discussion, to compromise by holding a party poll on the subject. The poll resulted in a three-to-two vote in Maxton's favour, which confirmed his dominance over the ILP. It appeared that the party needed Maxton more than it needed working-class sanctions against Italy.

Maxton's opposition to taking a strong stand over the invasion of Abyssinia was the outcome of his disenchantment with purely nationalist struggles. To qualify for his support nationalist movements had not only to seek to overthrow the colonial powers but also to identify with the aims of revolutionary Socialism. As he said in the *New Leader* (24 June 1932), the 'time has gone past for purely Nationalist struggles. A struggle for National independence and against imperialism can only be fully justified if it combines with it a struggle for the overthrow of capitalism as well'. This view became more entrenched as the 1930s wore on and nationalism became strongly associated with Fascism and Nazism. Because of this, Maxton's attachment to Home Rule for Scotland weakened condiserably. His last address under the auspices of the SHRA had taken place in 1928 and thereafter he became an opponent of the Scottish National Party. Nationalism in Scotland in the 1930s had, in fact, assumed a very right-wing stance with a number of prominent Nationalists openly supportive of Mussolini. Maxton's opposition to Scottish nationalism, however, continued beyond this period. He declared in 1943 that he repudiated the speech he had made twenty years previously in which he had asked for 'no greater job in life' than to free Scotland from English and other forms of domination. Abroad he opposed, as we have seen, Gandhi and the Indian Congress Party and threw his support behind the Indian Communists. In Palestine he opposed the Zionist calls for a homeland for Jews and instead advocated a united workers' state of Arabs and Jews and an end to British Imperialism there.

However, Maxton was hardly consistent or logical in his attitude towards Imperialism. While pointing to the fatal weakness in the League of Nation's approach and to the problems surrounding the imposition of working-class sanctions against Italy, to argue that there were no differences between the two sides in the Abyssinian War seems unbelievable. The extension of Imperialism through the annexation of Abyssinia weakened, not strengthened as Maxton imagined, revolutionary forces in the Third World. Moreover a defeat of Mussolini by whatever means would have destroyed the credibility of the Fascists in Italy and encouraged a Socialist back-lash. In the case of Eire, Maxton's views were even more inconsistent. After a visit to Eire in January 1934 with John McGovern, Maxton described De Valera as not a 'Socialist' but a 'great anti-Imperialist' and proceeded to attack the trade policy of the national government towards Eire.[31] However, if the purely national independence struggle was out of date, then how could Maxton lend his support to the De Valera government which, by his own admission, was not Socialist? Perhaps Maxton's policy towards Eire had something to do with the religious composition of the Bridgeton constituency. Not for the first time had the Irish Catholic presence in Bridgeton forced his hand on certain issues and produced an astonishing inconsistency in the application of Socialist theory to controversial social and political issues.

However, the major reason behind the contradictions in this aspect of Maxton's politics was his failure to realise the incompatibility of his philosophy of Socialism with Lenin's theory of Imperialism to which he ascribed. The former saw the world as one Capitalist state in which total capital exploited total labour; the other was more concerned with the disharmony of interests between sections of capital and the differences between the social and market positions of the workers. Imperialist theory saw colonial economies ruthlessly exploited by industrially developed nations to generate super profits, a sizeable proportion of which were used to buy the allegiance of the working class in the metropolitan power through an artificially high standard of living. Thus, in Lenin's view, colonial peoples were doubly exploited on the grounds of class and nationality. Any attempts by Nationalist movements to upset this process of exploitation would create a destabilisation of the economic and political structures of the Imperialist state by undermining its external sources of profit, eventually culminating in severe economic depression and revolution. It was these basic characteristics of the Leninist theory of Imperialism which Maxton failed to appreciate and which constituted the fundamental weakness in his application of it to Nationalist struggles – something which was also evident in his attitude to the civil war in Spain.

3

In June 1936 General Franco and other dissident military leaders serving in Spain's North African territories broke their oath of allegiance to the Republican government. The government of Spain was an alliance of 'progressive' forces and included Liberals, left Republicans, Socialists and Communists. It had incensed the army, church and right-wing extremists such as the Fascist Falange, by introducing a package of reforms intended to radically alter the traditional distribution of wealth and power in Spain. Agrarian reforms saw the break-up of the large landed estates and, in education, new legislation reduced the influence of the Catholic Church. The revolt against what was seen by the right as the creation of a secular workers' state soon spread to mainland Spain. In mid-July the Spanish rebel army, with the assistance of 30,000 Moorish troops, invaded southern Spain. Franco, who was receiving aid and support from Mussolini and Hitler, expected an easy victory but the largely untrained Republican militias held out in eastern and central Spain and retained control of the important cities of Barcelona and Madrid. The stubborn resistance of the Republicans meant that the war dragged on for three years. The eventual victory of Franco and the Spanish right signalled the beginning of the Second World War and this has led many historians to interpret the war in Spain as a dress rehearsal for the latter conflict.

From the outset, Maxton's attitude to the civil war in Spain was one of enthusiastic support for the Republican cause. He was prepared, as Tom Johnston noted, to fight with the International Brigade of British volunteers if he could have found a doctor to pass him fit. What made this struggle different to Maxton was that, unlike the Abyssianian War which he had labelled a Capitalist/Imperialist war, this was a workers' fight. However, why peasants and tribesmen fighting in Abyssinia against a Fascist regime should be treated differently from workers and peasants in Spain battling against similar forces was a question that Maxton never satisfactorily resolved. In spite of the tension in Maxton's position on this issue, the serious nature of the situation in Spain made theoretical consistency irrelevant. What the situation demanded was the total unity of the British left in support of the Republican forces.

Although the first United Front had collapsed in 1934, Maxton had never ruled out the possibility of future co-operation and unity if the conditions were right. In his Chairman's address to the 1935 ILP Conference, he said:

> I cannot say that I feel . . . that we are ready for unification of the ILP with the Communist Party. But I do feel that already things are shaping so that the possibility of the formation of a new working class party. . . with the ILP and the Communist Party as its central core is not in the far distant future but it is very near to us.

A further indication of his interest in unity on the left was the statement made during the 1935 General Election that he was prepared to work with the Communist and Labour Parties to defeat the national government, as long as it did not involve making compromises with agreed ILP policy. But his statement was proof that Maxton had failed to think the matter of unity through, as such an arrangement would inevitably have compromised ILP policy given differences in ideology. Furthermore, it was never made clear on what, or on whose terms, unity would take place. However, the events in Spain rendered these questions unimportant as the situation there demanded an urgent and unified response from the British Labour movement.

During the summer of 1936 negotiations to this end were conducted between the CPGB, the SL and the ILP, represented by Brockway and Maxton. The Communists argued for a popular front on the same lines as the French and Spanish but Maxton rejected this and instead called for the creation of a workers' front of proletarian parties. This view was shared by Cripps and Mellor of the SL and it formed the basis of the second United Front. The object of the Front was to force the Labour Party and the TUC, and through them the national government, to take positive measures to assist the Spanish government in its fight against the right-wing rebels. Another important part of its activities was to combat Fascism at home. This other objective achieved some success when the CPGB and, in a supporting role, the ILP and local London Labour parties managed to prevent a provocative march by Mosley's blackshirts by mobilising the East End working class on 4 October. The march was the culmination of a summer-long anti-semitic campaign by the BUF and thousands of workers turned out to demonstrate against the Fascists. A riot ensued and the police made repeated baton charges against the crowd to clear a path for the march. In the end the police advised Mosley to abandon the demonstration. The government's response was to pass the Public Order Act, which prohibited the wearing of political uniforms and empowered the police to ban marches if it was thought desirable. The new legislation was condemned by Maxton as leading Britain along the road to a 'one-party state'.

The 'Battle of Cable Street', as it became known, succeeded in radicalising the rank and file of the Labour movement and pressure was put on the Labour Party to adopt a more aggressive stand against Fascism. On 28 October Labour's NEC passed a resolution demanding the right of the Spanish government to buy arms. But, as it turned out, this was only a paper commitment. Both the Labour Party and the TUC refused to mobilise the workers in support of the demand as it was feared that to do so would heighten international tension. Labour's toothless support for the Republican forces in Spain was attacked on 21 November in a joint statement by Cripps and Mellor of the SL, Brockway and Maxton of the ILP and Gallacher and Pollitt of the CPGB. The national government's position of neutrality was also denounced. Speaking in the Commons debate on the Shipping (Carriage of Munitions to Spain) Bill in December 1936, Maxton accused the British government of refusing to assist the Spanish Republicans 'because of class prejudice'. As it was a government of the left, the Tories, Maxton claimed, had remained indifferent, if not actually hostile, to its fate.

So far the co-operation on the British left had only been informal. However, in January 1937 the *ad hoc* arrangement was abandoned and closer co-operation of policies and strategy was instituted. The key document in this process was the 'Unity Manifesto', which called for 'Unity in the struggle against Fascism, Reaction and War and against the National Government'. The manifesto included a number of easily agreeable demands such as the defeat of the national government, the abolition of the means test, improved scales of benefit for the unemployed, and so on. However, it also contained much of a controversial nature. Calls for a pact between the governments of Britain, France and the Soviet Union against Fascism and the unconditional return of a Labour government inevitably laid the basis for future disagreements among Front members, particularly given Maxton's antipathy towards gradualism and Capitalist/Imperialist wars. It was the actions of Labour's NEC which prevented an early doctrinal dispute in the United Front. On 27 January 1937 the NEC expelled the SL and almost immediately the Front began to fall apart.

Some members of the SL, most notably Cripps and George Strauss, continued to speak at unity meetings in spite of the ruling of Labour's Executive but in many ways the idea of left-wing unity was a fraud from the outset. As the war in Spain progressed, relations between the ILP and the CPGB deteriorated into hostility and mud-slinging. The main reason behind the growing bitterness between the Communists and the ILP was the latter's support for the Spanish Trotskyist organisation, the Patido Obrero de Unificacion Marxista (POUM), which advocated using the war to carry through a Socialist revolution, as against the Spanish Communist Party which argued that winning the war had to take precedence over revolution. The dependence of the Spanish government on Soviet military aid meant that the Communists were in virtual control of the state. They used their position to silence opposition from dissident groups in the Republican camp. Things came to a head when the Spanish government attempted to take control of the Barcelona telephone exchange from anarchists and POUM militiamen. Fierce fighting broke out behind the republican lines whch eventually led to the defeat of the POUM and the arrest of its leading members.

At the end of August 1937 Maxton, along with members of the French Socialist Party, the French League for Human Rights, the French Peasants' Party and Sneevliet of the Dutch Socialist Party, arrived in Spain to secure the release of condemned POUM leaders. The delegation was criticised by the Communist press in Spain, but, as Victor Serge, the veteran Russian revolutionary, recalled in his memoirs, the intevention of Maxton and Sneevliet was decisive in saving the lives of the POUM leaders. Maxton also intervened to save the life of Joachim Maurin, General Secretary of POUM, who had been condemned by Franco for his political activities before the Fascist uprising. Maurin was eventually released in 1946 and lived out the rest of his life in the USA.

On his return to Britain, Maxton walked into another controversy. Because of its support for the Spanish Republican cause, the ILP was bitterly denounced by the Catholic Church in Scotland. The *Glasgow Observer* (31 October 1936), the leading Scottish Catholic newspaper, singled out the ILP for special treatment, claiming 'No Catholic can be a member of the ILP because it is an avowedly Socialist organisation'. This opposition led to a fall in the ILP vote in municipal elections in Glasgow from 12.78 per cent of the poll in 1935 to 8.35 per cent in 1937. As part of a further attempt by the Catholic Church to discredit the ILP, it was claimed in his absence by the pro-Franco Catholic Union of Scotland that Maxton had been denounced by the Spanish Communists as 'a Fascist and an enemy of the working classes of Spain'. Indeed, the Secretary of the Spanish anarcho-syndicalist trades union, the CNT, Mariano Vazquez, wrote to Maxton on 25 August 1937 apologising for the insults hurled at Maxton and the ILP in some sections of the Spanish press. The full text of the letter appeared in the *New Leader* on 3 September. Maxton repudiated the claims of the Catholic Union as 'gross exaggeration', but admitted that his mission had provoked a hostile response from the Spanish Communist Party. For his part he said that he supported the maximum amount of working-class unity in Spain but he felt that solidarity was being undermined by the Communists, whose policy was 'not only vicious, but stupid'.[32] Maxton's criticisms of the Spanish Communists were buttressed by the reports of other ILP observers in Spain. John McGovern, ILP MP for Shettleston, published a book, *Red Terror in Spain* (1937), detailing Communist atrocities against their so-called anarchist and Trotskyist allies. Such sensational revelations destroyed whatever political bond there was between the two parties but the internal events in the Sovient Union also had a major influence in determining the rapidly declining relations.

During the period 1936-8 Stalin consolidated himself in power by liquidating any potential effective opposition to his leadership. Old Bolsheviks such as Kamanev and Zinoviev were shot in 1936 for being Trotskyists and plotting to assassinate Stalin. In 1937 Radek and eighteen others were executed for allegedly trying to restore Capitalism in the Soviet Union and for being agents of Fascist powers. The following year the leading Red Army generals and the one-time head of the Comintern – Bukharin – were also shot as Fascist agents. At first the 'show trials' stunned Socialists throughout the world but there was a general tendency to give Stalin the benefit of the doubt. In a review of Trotsky's *The Revolution Betrayed* (1937), Maxton was moved to attack the former for using the word 'betrayed' as it was inappropriate in judging men 'who, with the best will in the world, make mistakes'. But, as the trials continued, it became clear that Stalin was bent on a megalomaniacal drive for power and the mood changed. It seemed to Maxton and others that the purges in the USSR were an extension of the policies carried out in Spain by the Communists against their allies.

These events influenced Maxton to take a highly critical attitude towards Communist organisations and policies. Speaking at an ILP summer school in August 1937, he accused the CPGB of suppressing individual thought and action to such an extent that Communists were no longer 'capable of a free intellectual examination of the problems which face Socialists'. The following year he somewhat contradictorily, given what he was saying during the civil war in Spain, attacked the Communist idea of violent revolution by drawing an analogy with Russia before and after the October Revolution:

> the class struggle [has] to be maintained on the level of the struggle of the mind rather than brute force. . . I am convinced if it gets to the stage of a pitched battle, barricades in the streets, imprisonments, tortures. . . you will reproduce precisely the same things that have been produced in Russia. Russia, in destroying the tyrannies of the Czar, took onto itself many of the characteristics that the Czar. . . had displayed in. . . crushing the Russian people.[33]

Some months prior to Maxton's statement, the 'show trials' were condemned by the ILP in an open letter signed by NAC members on 9 March 1938. The letter spoke of the terror of the USSR and called on Stalin to put an end to it. This brought a stinging rebuke from the CPGB which, in a pamphlet written by Gallacher and entitled *The Dodgers: An Exposure and Criticism of the ILP* (1938), accused Maxton and the ILP of 'whitewashing Fascism'.

The CPGB reaction to the ILP's criticism of Stalinist excesses may also have been influenced by the seemingly pro-Trotskyist stance of the latter. The ILP had published articles by Trotsky in the *New Leader* in the 1930s and Maxton obtained a resident's permit to allow him to settle briefly in the Channel Islands. There was also the support of the POUM in the Spanish Civil War and Maxton and the ILP's condemnation of the Spanish Communists which further reinforced CPGB suspicions regarding the ideological soundness of the ILP. However, Communist suspicions were rather misplaced. Trotskyists had infiltrated the ILP in 1934 and won control of six London branches but their influence on policy was negligible and brief as by the end of November 1936 they had departed. Thus the differences between the ILP and the CPGB were the result of fundamental disagreements over the means and ends of Socialist activity and had nothing to do with schisms in the Third International

However, in these circumstances the idea of a United Front was a pipe dream. The differences in policy and the vision of Socialism, and the means of attaining it, between the ILP and the CPGB were too much to overcome. The situation was not helped by the expulsion of the SL from the Labour Party which undermined the second United Front before it really got going. The continued presence of the SL may have acted as a mediating force between the two warring parties but sooner or later the existence of profound ideological and political differences would have destroyed the Front. These differences progressively deepened in the period immediately before the outbreak of the Second World War as it became transparent that Maxton's political pacifism and commitment to the class struggle and opposition to progressive alliances constituted major barriers to a united left-wing demand for a pact between Britain, France and the USSR against the Axis powers. The ILP saw Fascism simply as a different political method of running Capitalism. Defeating Fascisms by military means did nothing to solve the major social and economic problems of Capitalist society, of which 'poverty' was the most important as far as Maxton was concerned. The task of Socialists, therefore, was to expose the war as one in which only the interests of the international ruling class were at stake, and to propagandise amongst the workers for social revolution. As a result, Maxton and the ILP found themselves increasingly isolated as the clamour for war reached fever pitch.

10 *The real thing*

1

The failure of the second United Front raised the question within the ILP of re-affiliation to the Labour Party. Undoubtedly the party had suffered significant losses of members and influence since 1932 and the practice of putting up accredited Labour candidates in ILP-held constituencies put all but Maxton's seat at risk. Early in 1938 a personal appeal was made by Cripps on behalf of Labour leader Clement Attlee to Maxton to rejoin the Labour Party. This was not the first time that overtures of this kind had been made. Arthur Woodburn, the Secretary of the Scottish Labour Party, recalled in his unpublished autobiography, *Some Recollections*, that Oliver Baldwin of the ILP had approached him in 1935 with a view to bringing the two parties together once more. As a result Woodburn wrote to Maxton saying that, if he were to give assurances, he would publicly invite the ILP to re-affiliate. Baldwin delivered the message to Maxton but the latter was dismissive, declaring that the Labour Party had plenty of 'fatted calves' for returning prodigal sons. Matters rested there until Cripps' intervention three years later. According to some sources, the second approach met with the approval of Maxton. Brockway in *Inside the Left* claims that Maxton was prepared to enter the Labour Party and accept parliamentary standing orders. This view is shared by ILP historian R. E. Dowse, who argued that Labour's decision to extend the conscience clause to allow ILP MPs to vote, if necessary, against the PLP removed the main obstacle to re-affiliation. In response to this concession from Labour, the NAC in 1939 decided to call a special conference for the purpose of recommending re-affiliation. However, war broke out and the conference had to be cancelled. But for that event it is clear, according to Dowse, that Maxton and the ILP would have returned to the Labour fold.

These views are somewhat overstated and, in Brockway's case, contradictory. Maxton may have been willing to work with Labour but at no time did he think of rejoining it. He always insisted that the ILP should retain its political freedom and independence and for the party to take a different course would, as Brockway noted in the sequel to the first volume of his autobiography, *Outside the Right* (1963), have 'cut him to the heart'. In spite of the election in 1945 of a Labour government elected on a programme not too dissimilar to SIOT, Maxton still opposed re-affiliation. Speaking at an ILP summer school in August 1945, he was asked the question 'Is the ILP still necessary?' and his reply presents a telling insight into how he felt about the re-affiliation issue:

> The objective of the ILP was not the creation of the Labour Party, but the establishment of a socialist order of society. The creation of the Labour Party was only an attempt to create an instrument which might achieve Socialism. It was not possible to assume that it was the final instrument . . . nor to accept that the ILP should wind up . . . we are not in the Socialist Commonwealth and until we are the ILP should maintain its organisation and carry on its work.[34]

As he remained convinced that the ILP still had an important role to play in the creation of a Socialist society, Maxton consistently voted against re-affiliation at all ILP conferences. Brockway, in a letter of resignation to Maxton written on 27 April 1946, makes it clear that Maxton had no thoughts of rejoining the Labour Party when he says 'I cannot conscientiously urge that the ILP should try to become an alternative to the Labour Party.' If this was Maxton's position in 1946, in 1938 his views were even more entrenched, as he felt that re-affiliation would impose restrictions on his anti-war activities. Moveover, the fact that those closest to him, his sisters and his son, remained in the ILP after his death would tend to confirm that he would have been unlikely to re-enter the Labour Party. The former's actions were as much a mark of respect to Maxton's memory as they were to do with political conviction.

2

The civil war in Spain was only part of the expansionism of the Fascist powers. The bellicose pronouncements of Hitler regarding *lebensraum* for the German peoples became shriller and more threatening in 1938 than at any previous time. On 12 March *Anschluss* with Austria was realised and Hitler began to turn his attention to the German-speaking peoples of the Sudetenland in Czechslovakia. The British government, under the leadership of Neville Chamberlain since May 1937, adopted a policy of appeasement towards the Fascist powers. Chamberlain was prepared to accept that the Germans had legitimate territorial grievances. The Treaty of Versailles had scattered the German people around eastern and central Europe and stripped Germany of its colonial possessions. This willingness by Chamberlain to concede that Germany had a case for reuniting the German peoples in one Reich was interpreted as a sign of weakness by the Fascist powers and was instrumental in leading to a series of diplomatic humiliations. Anthony Eden resigned as Foreign Secretary in February 1938 when Chamberlain agreed to talks with Mussolini without any assurance of good faith from the Italians. But this incident paled into insignificance after the humiliation of Munich later that year.

The situation in the Sudentenland was close to war and, to cool international feelings, Chamberlain arranged a meeting with the other members of the 'big four', that is, France, Germany and Italy. The talks were held at Hitler's retreat, the Berchtes-gaden, in September. During the negotiations Chamberlain agreed to the transfer, under the tripartite supervision of Britain, France and Germany, of the Sudetenland to the Germans and to revoke the terms of Versailles. Chamberlain interpreted the talks in an optimistic manner as a step forward in resolving international tensions. Before he left Munich he asked Hitler to sign a piece of paper which would indicate the determination of the two leaders to guarantee the peoples of Europe peace in their time. It was an act of incredible political naïvety, as Hitler had no intention of honouring the pledge, and the event did much to change the attitude of the British people to the prospect of war.

Much to the amazement of the British left and his own party, Maxton welcomed the Chamberlain mission for providing a 'breathing space' so that the forces of peace could exert pressure to remove the threat of war. Addressing the Commons on 4 October 1938, Maxton said, 'I congratulate the Prime Minister on the work he did in those three weeks'. The speech, however much Maxton tried to qualify it by claiming that the main thrust was directed towards the inevitability of war under Capitalism, created a storm of protest on the left. Willie Gallacher, of the CPGB stated that Maxton, in approving Chamberlain's actions, was endorsing 'the world's vilest act of treachery'. Within the ILP, criticism was no less fierce. Brockway published an article in the *New Leader* disassociating himself from Maxton's speech. There was also a demand by the Clapham branch that Maxton and those ILP MPs who had supported him be expelled from the party.

The first test of ILP opinion regarding Maxton's speech came at the Scottish Divisional Conference in Janauary 1939. A resolution moving back the report of the parliamentary group was after an emotional speech by Maxton, defeated by 12 votes to 62. However, a much sterner test lay ahead. At the Annual Conference of the ILP a strong attack was mounted against Maxton and the parliamentary group. The critics argued that Maxton had by his action underscored the folly of one of the 'most reactionary British Prime Ministers', who had made peace without regard to the interests of the working class; in other words, it was a Capitalist not a Socialist peace.

Although at odds with some of his party over Munich, Maxton was quite consistent in his attitude to war. To him wars were essentially economic in origin and were fought over the ownership and control of trade routes, markets and sources of raw materials. In spite of the rival ideologies involved, Maxton saw the Second World War primarily as the outcome of economic expansionism. It was the task of Socialists to oppose war, but not as pacifists. Maxton always resented being called a pacifist; he was anti-war not as a result of a Christian moralism but rather because wars were fought not in the interests of the poor but in the interests of the rich and powerful. The only effective way to abolish war was to do away with the causes of war which, in practice, meant the overthrow of Capitalism and the establishment of Socialism. In the absence of revolution there were, Maxton argued, a number of practical things workers could do to prevent the outbreak of international conflict. The Labour movments should oppose rearmament. Unilateralism had been advocated by Maxton since the First World War but in the tense atmosphere of the late 1930s this became multilateral disarmament. Maxton called on the international working class 'to develop the class struggle. . . to such an extent that it makes it impossible for any of the great Capitalist nations to think in terms of war'.[35] The Labour Party, TUC and CPGB were all attacked by Maxton for supporting the rearmament drive of the Chamberlain government.

Maxton was also concerned at the threat war posed to civil liberties and therefore opposed the introduction of conscription and the Official Secrets Act. During May 1939 he savaged the Military Training Bill as the only way Capitalism had of dealing with the problem of the industrial reserve army. The unemployed were to be wasted on the battlefield. Conscription, however, was seen only as part of a broader pattern of attack on democracy and dissent. The Official Secrets Act sought to silence government critics. Maxton had, in fact, been intimately involved at the committee stage of the legislation as a member of the select committee. He fought tenaciously against the Bill, arguing that there was no need to increase the already impressive legal powers of the state in dealing with crimes like sedition and treason. The legislation was also open to abuse as its interpretation lay solely with the state. Maxton, with remarkable insight, foreshadowed many of the criticisms to be made in the 1980s against the Official Secrets Act.

However, Maxton, with only a handful of supporters in the Commons, was monotonously defeated in his attacks on government policies. The Labour movement after the débâcle of Munich had swung solidly behind the struggle against Fascism and were to negotiate an industrial and political truce with the government once hostilities broke out. The Communists, formerly so enthusiastic for war with Germany, had, after the signing of the Nazi/Soviet pact in August 1939, gone through a period of intense inter-party debate lasting several weeks. At the outset of hostilities on 1 September they were still in favour of inflicting a military defeat on Fascism, with the *Daily Worker* proclaiming that 'The War is here. It is a war that CAN and Must be won'. Instructions from Comintern that the war was an 'imperialist' one changed this and by 12 October the *Daily Worker* was designating the Second World War as 'unjust and imperialist'. However, even with Communist support, the ILP was a voice in the political wilderness. Hitler, safe from attack from the east, invaded Poland and Chamberlain declared war on Germany.

Maxton associated himself in the Commons with George Lansbury's Parliamentary Peace Aims Group, which tried to put pressure on the government to negotiate a peace. In his opposition to the war Maxton had a rather unexpected ally in Beaverbrook. The latter had believed that there was little Britain could have done to aid Poland and that a strongly armed nation had nothing to fear from Germany. On 5 March 1940 he arranged a meeting with Maxton and the other ILP MPs at his mansion in London where he offered to give at least £500 to the ILP for every candidate they put up in wartime by-elections, and also offered all the resources of publicity at his command. But the ILP declined the offer of Beaverbrook gold, preferring to take their message direct to the workers. Beaverbrook's interest in pacifism was in any case only transient. By May that year he was Minister of Aircraft Production and pro-war. Meanwhile Maxton was speaking up and down the country on a number of platforms opposing the war, although he was always careful to stress that he did not mean by this 'surrender'. As he said to a meeting of 2,000 in Glasgow on 22 December 1940: 'I know for this movement against the war we have tremendous support – not mark you surrender. We have never suggested surrender; we suggest a conference. To make such a conference a possibility an armistice had to take place.'[36]

From his speeches and other interventions it was evident that he also thought that a situation would develop in Britain, as casualties mounted and hardship led to escalating industrial struggles, similar to those of the First World War. At a meeting of the ILP's NAC in August 1941, Maxton arrived at a naïvely optimistic assessment of the political situation. He claimed that 'the Socialist Revolution was the Revolution and Nazism the Counter Revolution; the thesis and the antithesis. The synthesis would appear and this would be our opportunity'. A year later this crude Marxism had changed to a form of wish-fulfilment, when Maxton declared: 'I believe the public mind will change as the war proceeds. We shall come to the point when the people will not only say that we are right but that they ought to have listened to us sooner.'[37]

As late as March 1944, when the prospect of defeat for the Allies had disappeared, Maxton was still deluding himself that 'anti-warrism would count in any election after the war'.

Perhaps this is an unfair judgement. There were grounds for optimism, given the leftward lurch of the British electorate during the war – a political trend reflected in by-election results. The ILP contested eleven constituencies during the war years and only lost its deposit once. It averaged around twenty to thirty per cent of the poll in by-elections in 1941 and in the first half of 1945 it nearly won two seats at Bilston and Newport. More remarkable were the successes of the Common Wealth Party (CWP) of Sir Richard Acland. It was formed in July 1942 when the war was going badly for the British. To win the war the CWP advocated moving Britain in a Socialist direction but after Tobruk this seemed unnecessary. The CWP began to campaign for the Beveridge proposals and for the common ownership of the land and industry, as well as improved moral and ethical standards in all spheres of public life. Interestingly, the party appealed to the middle classes in a big way, allowing it to win a small number of by-elections in formerly safe Tory seats. Thus there seemed to be a fusion of political radicalism and Socialism for a short time which may have given Maxton grounds for optimism but it was obvious that the small political parties were the recipients of the protest vote. The electoral truce between the major parties meant that there was no way that the electorate could express its dissatisfaction with the Churchill coalition government, other than by voting for fringe candidates. Once the war had been won and politics returned to normal, support for organisations like the ILP and the CWP fell away.

What Maxton failed to take into consideration when assessing the military/political situation were the essential differences between the First and the Second World Wars. The Second was waged against a Fascist alliance, the brutality of which was already notorious, whereas the First fitted more easily into the Imperialist/Capitalist rivalry thesis of the origins of war. Equally, in the Second, the state behaved much more responsibly in limiting profiteering and introducing rationing, thus promoting greater equality of sacrifice and avoiding the sort of criticisms that were raised, for example, by the Glasgow rent strikers during the First World War. In such circumstances it was difficult for Socialists to avoid the acute and real dilemma that Hitler had to be fought. The moral and political discontinuities between the two wars acted to isolate the anti-war movement; there was to be no repeat of 'Red Clydeside'. Although industrial relations were not always good, with 1,800,00 days lost in strikes in 1943 and a further 3,700,000 lost in 1944, these were mainly in the coal industry and in nine out of ten cases lasted less than a week. A communist-inspired Shop Stewards National Council was set up but, with the Soviet Union's entry into the war, it seemed to concentrate more on exposing 'inefficiency' at the workplace than in using the war to promote Socialist revolution among the workers.

In half-heartedly and ambiguously opposing the war, Maxton laid himself open to attack from his opponents in the Labour movement. At a by-election in 1939 in the Scottish constituency of Stirling and Clackmannanshire, Maxton spoke on behalf of the pacifist candidate. The local Labour Party put out a leaflet quoting Maxton's willingness to fight Fascism in Spain but not in Britain. A similar point was scored by Clement Attlee in a dabate with Maxton in the Commons on 5 December 1940.

Maxton called on the government to put forward peace proposals to bring the war to an end in order to re-establish the ideals of individual liberty and social justice. Attlee asked whether, if the government put forward peace terms with which Maxton agreed, he would support them. Maxton assured him: 'I certainly will', which provoked Attlee to ask further whether he would 'fight or give way', if Hitler refused to accept them. Maxton replied: 'I and my honourable Friends will not be found wanting'. On another occasion Attlee asked Maxton what he would do if Hitler invaded Britain? Yet again Maxton declared his resolve to resist Fascism by force if necessary, to which Attlee retorted, 'In these circumstances is it not better to tie them [Nazis] down across the Channel and thereby prevent them invading the country.'[38] For once Maxton was stuck for a coherent response. This kind of attack and the undoubted popularity of the armed struggle with the working class made his position extremely weak and, as the war progressed, Maxton became increasingly reticent. In late 1944 he fell silent when he collapsed and was forced to undergo a serious operation.

3

With the Allied invasion of the Continent, victory over Germany was assured. Political attention began to turn to the question of what kind of society Britain would be in the aftermath of war. One thing was agreed by all parties – there would be no return to the 1930s. Two reconstruction blueprints with their emphasis on social justice caught the imagination and mood of the British public – William Beveridge's report on social insurance and J. M. Keynes' policies for full employment. The idea of a welfare state was subscribed to by both Conservative and Labour Parties alike, but it was Labour whom the electorate most closely identified with it. Although Churchill was a popular war leader, his party was too strongly associated with the mass unemployment

of the inter-war years for the electorate to believe that the Tories
would introduce the package of reforms put forward by Beveridge
and Keynes. In any case, during the election campaign Churchill
saw winning the war against Japan as a greater priority than
setting up the welfare state. In was the failure of the Conservatives
to convince the electorate that they strongly supported the post-
war reconstruction blueprint of Beveridge and Keynes that sent
Labour into office with the largest majority any individual political
party had enjoyed.

On the whole, Maxton welcomed the election of the Attlee
government, but was sceptical concerning some of its legislative
proposals. Prior to falling ill in 1944, he, as a member of the
speaker's conference on electoral reform, was critical of the Representation of the People Act for not introducing proportional
representation and scrapping the £150 parliamentary election
deposit. In the same year he also attacked the heavily Keynesian
White Paper on employment policies. Although the document
formed the basis of Labour's post-war economic strategy, Maxton
saw it as a new version of Mond/Turnerism, providing the foundation of a consensus between labour and capital and nullifying
class antagonisms. At the same time it contradicted the Socialist
aim of returning to the worker the full fruits of his/her labour.
All the White Paper promised was work. As export-led economic
growth was also an important part of the Treasury's recipe for
recovery, Maxton criticised it as a plan to reduce wages. World
markets would only be won by undercutting the price of com-
petitor's goods, thus necessitating lower production costs, particularly wages. As the workers were suffering a reduction in
their standard of living, the Labour government, by generously
compensating the former shareholders of the new nationalised
industries, like coal and rail, was deliberately creating a rentier
class. It seemed to Maxton that Labour was rewarding capital at
the expense of labour.

However, in spite of these reservations, Maxton was prepared to endorse the Labour government. In a statement in the *New Leader* in August 1945 he said that the ILP would 'help in every way to make the Labour Government a success'. The following year he claimed that the Attlee government 'is something different in essence from anything we have ever had in this country'. Maxton especially welcomed the nationalisation of the Bank of England as it had been the 'money power which had destroyed the last Labour Government'. He was also supportive of Labour's plans to grant independence to India and endorsed the new social insurance reforms but he still did not consider re-affiliating to Labour. At the 1946 ILP Conference a resolution favouring re-affiliation was defeated by a narrow margin, with Maxton voting against it. However, by now there seemed little point in retaining a separate identity. Of the four ILP MPs; Buchanan resigned from the party in 1939 and was Minister of Pensions in the Attlee government, Stephen resigned after the 1945 general election and only McGovern remained loyal, probably out of respect for Maxton. However he too, eventually, found his way back to the Labour fold. Brockway got nearest to Maxton's reason for opting to stay outside the Labour Party when he wrote: 'Maxton understood the significance of Labour's victory. . . yet he could not identify himself with its government because it would have meant a denial of his prophetic vision.'[39] As always, Maxton was the idealist first and the politician second but one feels that, had he lived out the lifetime of the third Labour government, he would have looked at those years as something of a lost opportunity to change the social and economic face of Britain. Despite its reforming zeal the Attlee government failed to fundamentally alter the balance of power and wealth in society and by 1948 was bereft of imagination and policy.

4

Maxton's medical condition was increasingly deteriorating and this forced him to wind down his political activities. His last public meetings were in Barking, Motherwell and Hamilton; and his last appearance in the Commons was on 18 December 1945 where he proposed that an index should be included in the new weekly edition of *Hansard*. His final recorded public message was on the BBC's 'Good Cause' programme, where he appealed on behalf of the Glasgow Victoria Infirmary in which his son worked as a physician. His remaining months were spent with his wife Madeline at their home in Largs, Ayrshire. James Maxton died on 22 July 1946 of cancer, itself the result of a lifelong habit of chain-smoking and undernourishment. His staple diet was coffee and cigarettes. John McGovern recalled that one night in London during the blitz he smoked seventy cigarettes between 6pm and 8am. The funeral was held at Maryhill Crematorium, Glasgow, and was attended by people from all walks of life. Among the many floral tributes, there were wreaths from Churchill and Lord Beaverbrook. Sir Hugh Roberton of the Glasgow Orpheus Choir gave the funeral oration at what was a non-religious service.

Almost as soon as he died, tributes to Maxton's memory flooded in. The speaker of the Commons described him as 'a very remarkable and lovable colleague' and asked, and received, from the members of the House a few minutes silence to his memory. Fenner Brockway called him the 'greatest Briton of this generation both in his ideas and life', Lord Boyd Orr, of United Nations fame, claimed he was the 'greatest Scotsman of his age' and George Padmore, of the Pan African Federation, wrote: 'Maxton's memory will ever be cherished by Africans and peoples of African descent as the Wilberforce of his generation.'

Maxton was all of these things, and, at the same time, none of them. He was, in fact, a great contradiction. The essential qualities he possessed – socially, his humanitarianism and generosity of spirit and politically, his idiosyncratic brand of Marxian Socialism – were never unequivocal. His humour and good-naturedness endeared him to his supporters and opponents alike. Although opposed to Fascism, he found time to visit Mosley in Brixton Prison after he had been gaoled for his Fascist activities. Added to this was an integrity which was never in doubt. As Wheatley used to say, Maxton was the 'one man above suspicion' in the Labour movement. Yet the same man could be utterly contemptuous of his own party, as in 1929 when he made his ill-judged speech at the LAI Congress. Again, the humanitarianism could be misguidedly insensitive and naïve when seemingly at its most progressive. For example, Maxton championed the cause of penal reform but, in his ideal custodial establishment, he wanted murderers confined to a special unit where their brains could be studied. The irony of a humanitarian stripping other human beings of their dignity and self-respect never seemed to have occurred to Maxton.

The contradictoriness extended also to ideology and to politics. Maxton was a self-proclaimed follower of Marx, whose teachings, he once claimed, were the 'impregnable rock on which the working class movement laid the foundation of the new social system'. However, as a Marxist he was never consistent. Marx emphasised the role of class struggle in changing society, something to which Maxton subscribed but in his biography of Lenin he showed that he only possessed a very shallow understanding of Marx's theory of social change. According to Maxton, the Russian Revolution was carried through by Lenin with 'practically nothing but his own brain, his own will power and a theory'. The stress Maxton placed on the role of the individual in the dynamics of social change put him at odds with Marx's materialist conception of history. Indeed, Maxton admired 'great' individuals such as Keir Hardie and Lenin, particularly the latter, because he, unlike Marx, had resurrected 'the human element as the potent factor in social affairs'.[40] Similarly, Maxton's grasp of the essence of the Marxist/Leninist theory of Imperialism was inherently weak. It was inevitable, therefore, that such an unsound theoretical base would lead to inconsistency and contradiction – a feature of Maxton which was not remedied by his almost constant literary diet of cowboy and detective novels in his later years.

If Maxton was a great contradiction, was his life, as A. J. P. Taylor suggests, a 'wasted' one. Maxton's idealism made compromise, especially on points of principle, difficult. It was hard, therefore, to imagine him as leader of the Labour Party or a Cabinet minister. This is not to say that he did not possess leadership qualities. He could be extremely firm when the occasion demanded, as the RPC found to their cost in 1934, but he had an inflexibility about him which made it hard to tolerate people who were not going his way. Maxton also suffered from undue optimism regarding the willingness of the working class to accept his vision of social change. Time and time again he saw revolution round the corner and when events proved him wrong his belief remained as strong as ever. Moreover, the move to the left saw the ILP lodged between the CPGB and the Labour Party and there proved to be no alternative route between Stalinism and Social Democracy in the 1930s. Within this naïve hopefulness, however, there was a powerful critique made of existing institutions and the prevailing ideology and structure of the Labour Party. Maxton not only raised fundamental questions regarding the philosophy of gradualism, he also attacked the role of the trades unions in determining party policy and the power of the Cabinet and the PLP in deciding the actual legislation carried out by a Labour government. Maxton's aim was to thoroughly democratise the Labour Party and turn it towards a more radical vision of Socialism. This he found impossible to do. The power of the union bloc vote at conference and the genera conservatism of the Labour leadership effectively checked any attempt to defeat gradualism.

What Taylor and other critics fail to establish is how the ILP could remain an independent and influential force in the Labour Party in the face of these difficulties, given that the former was a declining party before Maxton became Chairman. Furthermore, the notion of 'waste' implies that, had he stayed in the Labour Party, Maxton would have realised his political potential as leader or minister of state. But since the critics have never spelt out exactly what that potential was and how, in the face of a highly conservative leadership in the Labour movment, he was to achieve high office, then this point remains obscure. In fact, Maxton was perhaps shrewder than he has been given credit for. In the politics of the 1930s he could do more to attack government policy and publicise Socialism as an independent agent than he could inside the imposed restrictions of the PLP's standing orders. As a member of the PLP he would probably have ended his political career as a tame backbencher, as did so many of the 'Red Clyde-siders'. As leader of the admittedly small ILP Maxton carved out a niche for himself in the public consciousness as a party leader and his skill in parliamentary debate won for his party the label of 'official opposition'. As Chairman of the ILP he commanded the centre stage of British political life for the best part of his career. This meant that he was able in no small way to affect the attitudes of the people towards unemployment and the injustices of government policy towards those out of work. In an indirect way such actions helped pave the way for the introduction of the welfare state at the end of the Second World War. A wasted life?

If we dispense with the prejudices of his critics and the hagiography of those who loved him, the one outstanding thing about Maxton's life which is instructive to the left in Britain today is the seeming impossibility of building an alternative to the cautious piecemeal approach of Social Democracy and the excesses of Stalinism. Maxton found in his failure that there was no middle way between the Labour Party and the CPGB. This pessimistic conclusion, however, should not blind us to the fact that his oratory and challenging idealism influenced thousands of young people to become Socialists and instilled in them a vision of Socialist society which transcended the narrow, unimaginative doctrines of Stalinism and State Capitalism. As long as the idea of 'Red Clydeside' and the world community of freely co-operative producers endures, then so will the name of Maxton, the 'incorruptible conscience' of the British left. His search for a Socialist/Humanist solution to economic crisis and war is as urgent today as it was in the 1930s.

Notes

1 A. J. P. Taylor, 'A wasted life?': a review of J. McNair's *James Maxton: The Beloved Rebel* (1955), in the *Observer*, 15 May 1955.

2. *New Leader*, 27 December 1941.

3. J. McNair, *op. cit.*, p. 24.

4. *Ibid.*, p. 53.

5. G. McAllister, *James Maxton: The Portrait of a Rebel*, 1935, p. 85.

6. *Glasgow Eastern Standard*, 3 May 1924.

7. McNair, *op. cit.*, p. 149.

8. M. Gilbert, *Plough My Own Furrow: The Story of Lord Allen*, 1965, pp. 194-5.

9. McNair, *op. cit.*, pp. 153-4.

10. F. Brockway, *Socialism over Sixty Years*, 1946, p. 324.

11. J. Paton, *Left Turn!*, 1936, p. 299.

12. NAC, *Minutes*, 30 June 1928.

13. *Sunday Worker*, 24 June 1928; L. J. MacFarlane, *The British Communist Party: Its Origins and Development until 1929*, 1966, p. 222.

14. *International Information*, LSI, VI, No. 28, 20 July 1929.

15. A. J. B. Marwick, 'James Maxton: his place in Scottish Labour history', *Scottish Historical Review*, XLIII, April 1964, p. 40.

16. *Inprekorr*, IX, No. 66, 29 November 1929.

17. *Hansard*, col. 1526, 12 March 1931.

18. A. Wooburn, 'Some Recollections', (Ms autobiography, Arthur Woodburn Papers, National Library of Scotland, Acc 7656), f. 76.

19. J. Scanlon, *The Decline and Fall of the Labour Party*, 1932, pp. 109-10.

20. A. J. P. Taylor, *Beaverbrook*, 1974, p. 421.

21. S. Cooper, 'John Wheatley: a study of labour history', Ph.D, Glasgow, 1973, pp. 366-7.

22. *Forward*, 27 April 1932.

23. G. D. H. Cole, *A History of the Labour Party from 1914*, 1948, p. 278.

24. T. Gallacher, 'Clash of 32', *Guardian*, 31 July 1982.

25. Marwick, *op. cit.*, p. 40.

26. *Glasgow Herald*, 7 January 1931.

27. *Everyman*, 16 March 1934.
28. *New Leader*, 24 August 1934.
29. *Hansard*, cols. 2073-5, 19 December 1935.
30. R. E. Dowse, *Left in Centre*, 1966, p. 195.
31. *Glasgow Herald*, 22 January 1934.
32. *Daily Herald*, 7 October 1937.
33. *New Leader*, 19 August 1938.
34. *Ibid.*, 1 September 1945.
35. *Ibid.*, 30 April 1937.
36. *Glasgow Herald*, 23 December 1940.
37. *New Leader*, 24 August 1942.
38. J. McGovern, *Neither Fear Nor Favour*, 1960, p. 155.
39. *Socialist Leader*, 3 August 1946.
40. *New Leader*, 31 December 1926.

Bibliography

Primary Sources

The James Maxton Papers have recently been bequeathed to the Strathclyde Regional Archives, Mitchell Library, Glasgow. The collection consists of letters, mainly written by others to Maxton, and voluminous press cuttings. Some important events in his political career are illuminated by the correspondence, especially his imprisonment during the First World War and his suspension from the House of Commons in 1923. But, on the whole, the collection is disappointingly thin. Other sources provide a better insight into his politics, particularly the weekly column he wrote for the *New Leader* in the late 1920s and early 30s. Among the many articles the following stand out as important: 'Mac-Donaldism, Communism and the ILP', 7 January 1927; 'What Next', 6 November 1931; 'Why socialists should be outside the Labour Party', 12 February 1932, and 'The new policy of the ILP', 18 August 1933.

In addition there are the published monographs and pamphlets, including *The Case of Benn v. Maxton*, 1929; *Lenin*, 1932; *If I Were A Dictator*, 1935; with A. J. Cook, *Our Case for a Socialist Revival*, 1928, 24pp.; with F. Brockway, *A Clear Lead*, 1932. *Hansard* also constitutes an important source, as do the *Minutes* of the NAC and his various addresses and contributions at ILP and Labour Party conferences. Not least is the massive amount of press reportage of his speeches and other political activities.

Bibliography

Secondary Sources

The existing biographies of Maxton – G. McAllister, *James Maxton: The Portrait of a Rebel*, 1935, and J. McNair, *James Maxton: The Beloved Rebel*, 1955, are highly partisan and, as such, fail to provide a balanced account of Maxton's career. McAllister's study is written from the Labour Party's point of view and highlights the indiscipline of Maxton and his followers whilst underplaying the failings of successive Labour governments. McNair's book is an exercise in hagiography, something which the author readily admits to. It is also disjointed, with an incoherent narrative. However, it contains a wealth of essential material on Maxton's youth and earlier political career. A more mature account is given by A. J. B. Marwick in 'James Maxton: his place in Scottish Labour history', *Scottish Historical Review*, XLIII, April 1964, but, at ninteeen pages, it is not a substitute for detailed historical biography.

Among the works on and by his contemporaries, F. Brockway's *Inside the Left*, 1942, and *Outside the Right*, 1963; D. Kirkwood's *My Life of Revolt*, 1935, and J. McGovern's *Neither Fear Nor Favour*, 1960, are all illuminating and basically sympathetic. S. Cooper's unpublished doctoral thesis 'John Wheatley: a study in Labour history', Glasgow, 1973, sheds a good deal of light on the Maxton/Wheatley relationship. More critical assessments are to be found in D. Marquand's *Ramsay MacDonald*, 1977, C. Cross, *Phillip Snowden*, 1966, M. Foot, *Aneurin Bevan: A Biography. Vol. 1: 1897-1945*, 1962, and E. Shinwell, *Conflict Without Malice*, 1955. More general political studies are also useful, not only as background but also for the sometimes perceptive observations on Maxton. R. E. Dowse's *Left in the Centre*, 1966, is essential reading on the history of the ILP, as is R. K. Middlemas' deeply flawed, but uniquely coherent account of inter-war Labour politics in Scotland, *The Clydesiders*, 1965. Still the best history of the Labour Party is G.

D. H. Cole's *A History of the Labour Party from 1914*, 1948, – a work which tries to understand the nature of and reasons for disaffiliation. The CPGB is an under-researched political party but what work had been done tends to be better handled by non-party members. L. J. MacFarlane, *The British Communist Party. Its origin and development until 1929*, 1966, is impressive, less so is J. Klugmann, *History of the Communist Party of Great Britain* Vol. 1, 1968, and Vol. 2, 1969, and N. Branson's *History of the Communist Party of Great Britain 1927-1941*, 1985. Specific aspects of Maxton's political philosophy, such as nationalism, are well treated in M. Keating's and D. Bleiman's *Labour and Scottish Nationalism*, 1979. For birth control see D. Russell, *The Tamarisk Tree*, 1977, and for involvement with the LAI see Labour Party's Report on the LAI (ID/C1/36). A large collection of biographical studies of Maxton's Scottish contemporaries can be found in W. Knox (ed.), *Scottish Labour Leaders, 1918-1939: A Biographical Dictionary*, Edinburgh, 1984.

Index